Keeping the FAITH
in a Rapidly Changing World

ANCIENT LANDMARKS AND BOUNDARIES

Pastor Lillian A Orinda

Copyright

Copyright ©2023 **Keeping the Faith in a Rapidly Changing World: Ancient Landmarks and Boundaries**

by **Pastor Lillian A Orinda**

All rights reserved. No part of this publication may be reproduced, stored in a retrieval system or be transmitted in any form or by any means, mechanical, electronic, photocopying or otherwise without the prior consent of the copyright owner.

Unless otherwise stated, Bible Scriptures are taken from the New King James Version®. Copyright © 1982 by Thomas Nelson. Used by permission. All rights reserved.

Scriptures marked (KJV) are taken from the King James Version (1611, 1769, Oxford University Press, Public Domain).

Scripture marked (NIV) are taken from THE HOLY BIBLE, NEW INTERNATIONAL VERSION®, NIV® Copyright © 1973, 1978, 1984, 2011 by Biblica, Inc.® Used by permission. All rights reserved worldwide.

Formatting and interior design: Dr Jacqueline N Samuels
https://tinyurl.com/AuthorJNSamuels

Cover design by Serve and Thrive:
https://tinyurl.com/SelfPublishSnT

ISBN: 9798387509797

Visit us at **https://newlifedbc.org/**

Contents

Copyright iii
Dedication v
Acknowledgements vi
Endorsement viii
Foreword xi
Introduction xii
Chapter One: Understanding the Prodigal Journey 1
Chapter Two: God Loves Us All 9
Chapter Three: The Prodigal Believers 15
Chapter Four: Who is a 'Believer'? 24
Chapter Five: The Lost and Found Parables 34
Chapter Six: The Promise to the Church 45
Chapter Seven: Misplaced Priority 52
Chapter Eight: Prodigal Praise and Worship 57
Chapter Nine: Change into Garments of Honour 65
Chapter Ten: Heeding God's Voice 73
Chapter Eleven: How Can We Return to the Father? 85
Chapter Twelve: Restoring our Focus on Christ 92
Chapter Thirteen: Prodigal Believers Link to the Parables 100
Chapter Fourteen: The Glorious Church 108
Chapter Fifteen: Return to Your First Love 114
Conclusion 124
About the Author 128

Dedication

This book is dedicated to God for His loving kindness and tender mercies. Holy Spirit, my Faithful Guide: Thank You for inspiring me to write this book and giving me a message about the Body of Christ.

To my husband for inspiring me on this journey: I appreciate our ministry walk in guiding souls to follow Christ. God bless you.

To every believer and all who are reaching out to the lost with open arms: your ministry represents Christ's heart for the hurting who are searching for the way back to the Father's embrace.

May our Creator richly reward your dedication and faithful service in His Vineyard.

Acknowledgements

Holy Spirit, this book would not have come to light without Your constant guidance and breath of life. Thank You for being my constant Friend along life's journey.

Special thanks go to my husband Reverend Walter Orinda for believing in me and continuously encouraging me to write and share what the Lord has instilled in my spirit. Your immense wisdom has helped shape this book. I love you, my friend and co-worker in the Lord's Vineyard.

To my son Sammy: thank you for taking time from your busy schedule to cheerfully help with typing the first draft of this book.

Apostle Marjorie Esomowei: thank you for encouraging me to just "*Go for it*." I took your advice, and the fruit is now evident. God bless you for the insight you shared along the way.

Special thanks to Reverend William Boyd for believing in me and allowing my light to shine. Your constant encouragement, mentorship and prayers have eased the journey. We need more spiritual father figures like you.

New Life Destiny Baptist Church family, friends, associates and my family members: I appreciate you all for your tireless support and encouragement.

I am indebted to my editor and book publishing coach Dr Jacqueline Samuels. Thank you for guiding me through the entire writing journey. Your attention to detail helped to ensure the message flowed with clarity and ease. In you I have found my destiny helper. God bless your work.

Pastor Oyinlola Bukky Akande (Oba), you told me to *"just start writing."* How true! The words effortlessly wove their way to life after the first line. I appreciate you.

Gratitude to Pastor Timothy and Pastor Justice who spoke life to this book by faith.

Apostle Jane Kiguru, deepest appreciation for your prayerful support, insight and wisdom through the final stages of this book.

I am grateful for everyone who has cheered me on throughout this writing journey. God bless you all.

Pastor Lillian Orinda

New Life Destiny Baptist Church

https://newlifedbc.org/

Endorsement

This Book is clearly born out of a walk with the Lord alongside being mentored by strong godly men and women who have a passion to see revival in the church. Not many people in this category are focused on the church of God taking its place in this end time.

Looking at prodigals through the eyes of God's love is deeply liberating and empowering. In **Keeping the Faith in a Rapidly Changing World** Pastor Lillian provides an extensive two-fold blueprint:

1. How to recognise a prodigal believer and
2. How the church can see herself and run back to God.

In this Book you will experience God's love afresh and thereby become part of the remnant who are encouraging the return of our Lord Jesus Christ.

The *Reflection* activities to ponder and complete in every chapter are very empowering and engaging. The readers' involvement in this Book consistently ensures that this book is not only read but worked on to become a reality.

You will constantly be redirected back to God's heart and ways which in turn will enable you to embrace a much-needed lasting transformation within the body of Christ.

This write-up serves as an instructional guide with multiple uses. The strategies emphasised within will encourage the church back if we would just read digest, reflect, and act upon the nuggets shared within.

I feel very privileged to have been accorded the opportunity to endorse this life-changing book.

Pastor Oyinlola Bukky Akande

Write your vision, make it plain...

Foreword

From the beginning to the end of the book, the reader continues to get revelations about how to thrive *in a Rapidly Changing World*.

Pastor Lilian skilfully and biblically gives us some concrete guidelines that would enable us manoeuvre through current and upcoming life world events.

I consider this book very sound, relevant and a helpful tool for believers to overcome present day challenges. The book activates the spiritual hunger of the reader and clearly reveals God's heart for the end time Church.

In this era of fear, lack of commitment and misplaced priority, Pastor Lilian offers us some solid solutions and principles to keep us in the path of victorious Christian living.

Are you a matured Christian? This book is for you.

Are you a growing Christian? This book is for you.

Are you a Ministry Leader? This book is for you.

Are you an aspiring Ministry Leader? This is a definite read.

Congratulations Pastor Lillian on a very apt and life transformational book. God bless you.

Apostle Marjorie Esomowei

Author, Life Coach, Prayer Strategist

Introduction

This book has been marinating within me since 2008 when I was first made aware of the mystery of the Prodigal believer within the changing church dynamics.

The journey started as a daily devotional I was inspired to share with work friends. After reading a Scripture I would ask listeners what they thought about it. Their varied responses struck a chord, and I started taking notes.

As we expound on the *Lost and Found* Parables revealed in Luke chapter 15, we will uncover how the church can return to the body of Christ and realign with the ancient landmarks and boundaries set for His children before the foundations of the world. Those who are called by God need to be rightly positioned so that they will be the instruments of restoration God will use in the constantly changing world.

Many Christians have lost their bearings and focus in terms of having consistent fellowship with God. The desire for temporal worldly pleasure has derailed many believers, forgetting that seeking fellowship with the world removes them from the grace of God.

It is my sincere desire that we will mindfully and prayerfully read what the Word of God says about the need to restore lost believers back to the heart of a loving Father.

It is our joint responsibility as leaders, followers of Christ, evangelists, pastors, church visionaries, parents and worshippers to do our part in Kingdom building so that no soul will be lost in these last days.

This is an interactive experience. At the end of every chapter, you will have a reflection activity to ponder and complete prayerfully. The aim is to create a lasting transformation in your Christian walk with the LORD through this book.

You can use this instructional guide in your Bible study and home study sessions, quiet reflections, individually or with family members. Refer to the topics often as you progress along your journey.

Let's get started.

Chapter One:

Understanding the Prodigal Journey

Any non-believer can eat or do anything they like and not feel guilty. By contrast, the believer considers their actions and is mindful of possible repercussions.

Let us begin by identifying several terms we will be using in this book namely, *prodigal, believer, prodigal believer,* and the *non-believer.*

*What do we mean by **prodigal**?*

Luke 15 introduces three scenarios of 'lost and found' believers, describing them as **prodigals**. The same term is described in various ways. For example, the Webster-Merriam dictionary terms a **prodigal** person as one who loves to spend money or use resources freely and recklessly, and a wastefully extravagant person.

Other descriptions include spendthrift, improvident, imprudent, immoderate, profligate, thriftless, excessive, intemperate, irresponsible, self-indulgent, reckless, wanton.

A *prodigal person* may also be referred to as having or giving something on a lavish scale. Using this description, one is deemed to be generous, lavish, liberal, unstinting, unsparing, bountiful, copious, profuse, abundant in, rich.

Prodigal people are not concerned about nurturing what they have not worked hard for. They like to be known for their generosity which translates to recklessness, wasteful high class living, and extravagance by living above one's means. Mindless extravagance leads to poverty and lack, and ultimately, regret.

*Who is a **believer**?*

The Oxford Dictionary defines a **believer** as a person who believes in the truth or existence of something; they believe that a specified thing is right, effective, or acceptable:

In terms of one's faith: one who adheres to a particular religion. This may also refer to God inviting believers into a relationship with Himself. A **believer** is seen as one devoted to a person or faith, disciple of, follower of, supporter of, upholder of, worshipper in, convert, born-again.

Christians often refer to a **believer** as one who is **born-again**. Some Christian songs have incorporated these terms in the lyrics to identify the believer's faith walk with God.

*Who is a **prodigal believer**?*

Within the context of this book, we will define a ***prodigal believer*** as a Christian or believer in God who goes off to live a lavish life aimed at pleasing the flesh and soul. The ***prodigal believer*** is not concerned with following what the Word of God says about righteous living that pleases

Him. Whatever the ***prodigal believer*** feels they want to do, wherever they want to go, they follow their heart's desires with no consideration of the consequences. Possible repercussions are furthest from the ***prodigal believer's*** mind.

Christians are at the crossroads in a rapidly changing world where we are constantly bombarded with conflicting messages from daily news networks, social media, other faiths and more. The challenge facing the modern church is how the prodigal believer can return to the ancient path God set for those who choose to believe and follow His Word. Jeremiah 6:16 decrees,

> *Thus says the Lord: "Stand in the ways and see, and ask for the old paths, where the good way is, and walk in it; then you will find rest for your souls. But they said, 'We will not walk in it.'*

God has already ordained the path that will ensure stability and focus in following His precepts. However, the sensory overload many young believers face blurs their vision causing them to forgo an eternity with Christ at the expense of temporary earthly enjoyment.

In the following chapters, we will examine some ***prodigal believers*** and identify signs of the same within the church environment. We will also explore steps we can take to restore them back to the fold. The parable of *The Lost Sheep* is normally preached in demonstration of a soul returning to God in repentance.

Ancient Landmarks and Prodigal Believers

Many have spoken of the prodigal church, which is evident in our current world. The church has gone astray and has not hearkened to the Voice of the Lord. Eli the prophet understood the importance of preserving the ancient landmarks. When he warned his two sons Hophni and Phinehas about the dangers of their wicked ways, they did not listen to him. Following their disobedience, four members of Eli's family were destroyed in one day.

Phinehas' wife died after giving birth to a bouncing baby boy who she named **Ichabod** which means *the glory has departed*. 1 Samuel 4:10-11 relates the story that prompted this child to be given such an unfortunate name.

One day the Israelite army met the Philistine army in battle; the Israelites thought it a good idea to bring the Ark of the Covenant along, hoping it would bring them good fortune. Eli's sons Hophni and Phinehas accompanied the Ark. However, since God's blessing was not on the endeavor, the Philistines won the battle. They killed Eli's two sons and captured the Ark of God.

Eli tried to remain strong when he learnt that his two sons had been killed in battle. However, when the bearers of the news told Eli that the Ark of God had been captured by the Philistines, he was overcome with grief. At that point he fell over backward, broke his neck, and died. This reveals how important the Ark of God was to Eli and the Israelite army camp.

1 Samuel 4:19-22 records,

> *Now his daughter-in-law, Phinehas' wife, was with child, due to be delivered; and when she heard the news that the ark of God was captured, and that her father-in-law and her husband were dead, she bowed herself and gave birth, for her labor pains came upon her. And about the time of her death the women who stood by her said to her, "Do not fear, for you have borne a son." But she did not answer, nor did she regard it. Then she named the child Ichabod, saying, "The glory has departed from Israel!" because the ark of God had been captured and because of her father-in-law and her husband. And she said, "The glory has departed from Israel, for the ark of God has been captured."*

Meanwhile, Eli's daughter-in-law, Phinehas' wife, was about to give birth. When she heard that her husband and father-in-law had died, she went into labor. With her dying breath she named her child **Ichabod**, because "*the glory has departed from Israel.*" The capture of the Ark of God must have deeply disturbed Phineas' wife and Eli because they recognized the significance of the Ark of God residing among their people.

When we step out of God's glory, we cannot win any victory. The children of Israel were presumptuous when they took the Ark of God into the battlefield before consulting the Almighty. Although the Ark of God was with them in the battlefield, His Glory had departed from them. As a result, the Philistines encouraged themselves and defeated the Israelite army who incurred many losses.

Had the children of Israel sought God's wise counsel on the matter before going to fight the Philistine army with the Ark of God, four members of Eli's family would not have lost their lives that day.

The modern Church is living a prodigal believer's lifestyle. Consider the following: prodigal preaching and teaching of God's Word, prodigal fundraising and manipulation, prodigal lifestyle, hatred and jealously, deception, to prodigal church members and leaders.

As the Church of Jesus Christ, we need to set our hearts right before God so that we will be restored to His intended glory as the righteous Body of Christ. Let us discover how to guide the lost Christians back to our Creator's ancient landmarks and pathways in the following pages.

This is what the Lord says: "Stand at the crossroads and look; ask for the ancient paths, ask where the good way is, and walk in it, and you will find rest for your souls. But you said, 'We will not walk in it.'

(Jeremiah 6:16)

Time to Reflect:

Growing in faith takes daily commitment.

Name one challenge you have experienced in your faith journey.

How did you overcome?

Chapter Two:
God Loves Us All

"Behold what manner of love the Father has bestowed on us, that we should be called children of God!"

(1 John 3:1)

No kind of love can be compared with the love Jesus gave us. No friend can lay down their lives and freely die for us.

There is a festival holiday called 'Valentine's Day', also known as 'Love Day'. Looking beyond the physical, we need to see this day as a day to talk to people about God's love for humanity. No man can express the love of their 'Valentine' more than the Love of God, because He gave His only Son to die for us. The sweetest words you might receive on Valentine's Day cannot extend to the point where the person is willing to lay down their life for you.

Born-again Christians are born into the family of God which makes us *believers in God*. When we repent of our sins we are *converted* into the family of God. We gain new identities as children of God when we invite Jesus Christ to live in our hearts. *Repenting* involves saying *sorry* to God for the many wrong things we have done in our lives. *Worshipping God* is an integral part of the believer's Christian growth. We will further explore the power of *worship* in a later chapter.

Sometimes believers fall away from following the precepts God has laid out in the Holy Bible. Born-again believers become **prodigal believers** when we stop obeying God's instruction or structure revealed in His Word. However, we are restored to our rightful position in Christ when we embrace the love of God.

We need to go back to the crossroads as Jeremiah 6:16 (NIV) declares:

> *This is what the Lord says: "Stand at the crossroads and look; ask for the ancient paths, ask where the good way is, and walk in it, and you will find rest for your souls. But you said, 'We will not walk in it.'*

Many have chosen not to listen to the Lord's wise instruction, choosing instead to go their own way and do as they please. We need to return to God. The Book of Genesis 3:9 reveals: *And the Lord God called unto Adam, and said unto him, "Where art thou?"*

Today God is asking the Church the same thing: *Where are you?* Ponder the following questions:

- *Are you that individual of whom people can confidently say you are a witness for Christ?*
- *Are you living by the Word of God or by the world's standards?*

- *Are you displaying Christ's character and love in your daily walk?*

Within the Body of Christ:

- *How long are we intending to do the same things without achieving the desired results?*
- *For how long will we continue to commit the same sins? Are we taking the grace of God for granted?*

Romans 6:1-2 asks: *What shall we say then? Shall we continue in sin that grace may abound? Certainly not! How shall we who died to sin live any longer in it?*

The major question then is:

- *Are we being led by the Spirit of God or by the flesh?*

We need to define whether we are Kingdom seekers or fence-sitters. What should we do to make a difference like some of the people we know as God's generals did for the Kingdom of God?

I have been asking myself a lot of questions, including: **Where is the Body of Christ headed in today's fast-changing world?**

If you were a non-believer, would you really admire your lifestyle as a Christian?

God is asking where the Church is.

Are you in the right place at the right time?

Let us reason together as a Church, as we seek after a lasting solution to the issues surrounding us, for we are truly at the cross-roads.

Time to Reflect:

Are you a witness for Christ?

Are you living by the Word of God or by the world?

How are you displaying Christ's character and love in your daily walk?

> You shall love the Lord your God with all your heart, with all your soul, and with all your strength.
>
> (Deuteronomy 6:5)

Chapter Three:
The Prodigal Believers

The Prodigal Believer is described as a person whose life is going beyond limits and living a wasteful life. The person lives with no responsibility and can be marked as someone who loves lavish living without living right by God's standards.

The *prodigal son* had no reason to move out from the father's home, he simply wanted to have his inheritance ahead of time. In other words, he wanted to discover what his father's will was between himself and his brother.

Prodigal believers want to live like unbelievers. They always have excuses, always want to outshine everyone, and complain often about tiny inconsequential things. Prodigal believers do not feel good if they do not complain. No department in the company is good; what they say is always right in their own eyes. They don't accept correction and whatever they say is final, whether it is true or not.

Prodigal believers have unrealistic expectations, and often live in a fantasy world. For example, a young lady meets a suitable man who treats her lavishly during their courtship period. After they get married, the woman expects the same treatment, giving no thought to related expenses, without expecting to contribute towards a happy union going forward.

This type of believer often has a hidden agenda and before long, one will hear them talking of how God is leading them to start a church. This results in a prodigal start of a faulty foundation.

Where did this erroneous way of living stem from? Let us now examine God's redemption plan for all humanity.

The First Adam and the Last Adam

In 1 Corinthians 15:45-47 (NKJV), Paul the Apostle spoke of the first Adam and the second Adam.

> *And so it is written, "The first man Adam became a living being." The last Adam became a life-giving spirit. However, the spiritual is not first, but the natural, and afterward the spiritual. The first man was of the earth, made of dust; the second Man is the Lord from heaven.*

Adam's purpose was to have a relationship with God while Jesus was to reconcile us back to God. Apostle Paul expresses that Adam was from the ground, and anyone that is from the ground speaks of earthly matters. However, Jesus was from above. Paul further states that He (Jesus) who came from above is greater than all.

Luke 15:1-2 recounts how the tax collectors and sinners all gathered to hear Jesus teach. When the Pharisees and Scribes murmured and wondered why Jesus was the centre of attention, He decided to explain His mission on earth to His hearers. This is how the Parables of The Lost Sheep, The Lost Coin and The Prodigal Son came about.

"Then all the tax collectors and the sinners drew near to Him to hear Him. And the Pharisees and scribes complained, saying, "This Man receives sinners and eats with them."

Before this day, Jesus returned into Galilee by the Holy Spirit's power, after spending forty days fasting and praying in the wilderness. Luke 4:14-16 relates how Jesus' ministry began.

Then Jesus returned in the power of the Spirit to Galilee, and news of Him went out through all the surrounding region. And He taught in their synagogues, being glorified by all. So He came to Nazareth, where He had been brought up. And as His custom was, He went into the synagogue on the Sabbath day, and stood up to read.

Jesus was accustomed to worshipping in the Synagogue on the Sabbath day. He explained what Prophet Isaiah had prophesied about Him. Luke 4:17-19 echoes Prophet Isaiah's words revealed in Chapter 61:1-2.

And He was handed the book of the prophet Isaiah. And when He had opened the book, He found the place where it was written: **"The Spirit of the Lord is upon Me because He has anointed Me to preach the gospel to the poor;**

He has sent Me to heal the brokenhearted, to proclaim liberty to the captives and recovery of sight to the blind, to set at liberty those who are oppressed; to proclaim the acceptable year of the Lord." (Emphasis mine)

What do we learn from the previous passage?

- The Spirit of the Lord was on Jesus. He advised His disciples to wait until the Holy Spirit came upon them at Pentecost (Acts 1:8).

- He was anointed to preach the gospel to the poor in spirit (that is, a humble heart, see Matthew 5:3; also God opposes the proud and gives grace to the humble -James 4:6)

- He was sent to heal the broken-hearted. Psalm 147:3 declares, *He heals the brokenhearted and binds up their wounds.* Further, Psalm 51:17 states: *The sacrifices of God are a broken spirit, a broken and a contrite heart—These, O God, You will not despise.*

- His mission was to preach deliverance to the captives and recovery of sight to the blind. Ephesians 1:17-18 calls us to embrace God's unfailing wisdom that opens our spiritual eyes:

  That the God of our Lord Jesus Christ, the Father of glory, may give to you the spirit of wisdom and revelation in the knowledge of Him, the eyes of your understanding being enlightened; that you may know what is the hope of His calling, what are the riches of the glory of His inheritance in the saints...

Furthermore, once your eyes of understanding are enlightened, you realise that you are not meant to be in captivity, as revealed in Daniel chapter 9.

- He came to earth to set at liberty all who were bruised (see also Luke 4:18). Psalm 126:1-2, 5 describes the reward of those who God sets at liberty:

When the Lord brought back the captivity of Zion, we were like those who dream. Then our mouth was filled with laughter, and our tongue with singing. Then they said among the nations, "The Lord has done great things for them." Those who sow in tears shall reap in joy.

- He was called to preach the acceptable year of the Lord. 2 Corinthians 6:2 expounds this truth: *For He says: "In an acceptable time I have heard you, and in the day of salvation I have helped you." Behold, now is the accepted time; behold, now is the day of salvation.*

The above Scriptures clarify Jesus' assignment which was to bring recovery of sight (Coin) to the blind; that is our connection back to God the Father. Jesus was the only One assigned and qualified to restore us back to God.

Who is the Church?

Matthew 16:13-18 states,

> *When Jesus came into the region of Caesarea Philippi, He asked His disciples, saying, "Who do men say that I, the Son of Man, am?" So they said, "Some say John the Baptist, some Elijah, and others Jeremiah or one of the prophets." He said to them, "But who do you say that I am?" Simon Peter answered and said,* ***"You are the Christ, the Son of the living God."*** *Jesus answered and said to him, "Blessed are you, Simon Bar-Jonah, for flesh and blood has not revealed this to you, but My Father who is in heaven.* ***And I also say to you that you are Peter, and on this rock I will build My church, and the gates of Hades shall not prevail against it.*** (Emphasis mine)

On this occasion, Jesus wanted to know if the disciples understood who He was by asking them what others were saying about Him. In response to the direct question, *"Who do you say I Am?"* one of his disciples, Peter, answered He was Christ, the Son of the living God.

The Bible says in Romans 10:9, *"that if you confess with your mouth the Lord Jesus and believe in your heart that God has raised Him from the dead, you will be saved."* Peter believed and therefore confessed, then Jesus acknowledged Peter's confession (Matthew 16:16-18).

In the above passage, Jesus spoke about the Church for the first time. We understand that when an individual confesses Jesus as Lord and Saviour, this makes the believer the Church. Many believe that the building is the church but to my understanding the building is where the Body of Christ assemble or meet for fellowship.

Reflect on the above conversation between Jesus and His disciples and answer the following questions.

Time to Reflect:

Who is Jesus in your life?

Have you confessed that Jesus is Lord in your life? If not, say this prayer.

Sinner's prayer

Dear God, I am a sinner and need Your forgiveness. I believe that Jesus Christ shed His precious blood and died for my sins. I am willing to turn from sin. I now invite Jesus Christ to come into my heart and life as my LORD and personal Saviour. Amen.

Did you pray the above prayer?

If you answered YES, welcome to the family of God! You are now a believer who seeks the heart of God. Read on to discover how to stay in tune with God's plan for your life.

"If you confess with your mouth the Lord Jesus and believe in your heart that God has raised Him from the dead, you will be saved."

(Romans 10:9)

Chapter Four:

Who is a 'Believer'?

The Apostle Peter defines a believer in 1 Peter 2:9-10 (KJV):

> *"But ye are a **Chosen** generation, a **Royal** priesthood, a **Holy** nation, a **Peculiar** people; that ye should shew forth the praises of him who hath called you out of darkness into his marvellous light; which in time past were not a people but are now the people of God: which had not obtained mercy, but now have obtained mercy."* (Emphasis mine)

Following Christ's sacrifice on the Cross, we are now the people of God who have received His mercy. We serve a loving God who has redeemed us and called us into His everlasting Kingdom!

Exodus 19:5-6 declares:

> *"Now therefore, if you will indeed obey My voice and keep My covenant, then you shall be a special treasure to Me above all people; for all the earth is Mine. And you shall be to Me a kingdom of priests and a holy nation. These are the words which you shall speak to the children of Israel."*

Thank God who always confirms His Word and makes known His heart to all who will hear and obey Him.

The Shepherd and the Sheep

John 10:14-15 tells us that Jesus is the Shepherd, and we are the sheep. Verse 14 states, "*I am the good shepherd; and I know My sheep, and am known by My own.*"

Let us now reflect on Jesus's words in John 10:27 "*My sheep hear My voice, and I know them, and they follow Me.*" Whose voice do you listen to? Some follow influencers on Instagram, Facebook, and other social media platforms; who is your greatest influencer? *Who do **you** follow?*

The true Shepherd is Jesus Christ, Son of the Living God. When you choose to follow Him, you will never go astray (v28): "*And I give them eternal life, and they shall never perish; neither shall anyone snatch them out of My hand.*"

Since the sheep know the Voice of the Lord, they do not follow the voice of a stranger (John 10:4-5, NKJV).

> *And when he brings out his own sheep, he goes before them; and the sheep follow him, for they know his voice. Yet they will by no means follow a stranger, but will flee from him, for they do not know the voice of strangers.*"

While David was taking care of his father's flock, he protected the flock from harmful animals. His experience caused him to write in Psalm 23:1, *"The Lord is my shepherd, I shall not want."* David likened everything did for his father's flock as service to the Lord.

John 21 records how Peter decided to go fishing. The other disciples also followed him, demonstrating that Peter was an influencer. Although they were all seasoned fishermen, they failed to catch any fish despite toiling all night. When Jesus arrived the following morning and asked them to throw their nets on the right side, this time Peter did not say *"we've toiled all night."* The disciples chose instead to obey Him and caught a lot of fish. After breakfast Jesus had a conversation with Peter, reminding him that he should be a **fisher of men** rather than a **fisher-man**.

That day the disciples learnt a vital lesson: that obeying Jesus's Word led to tangible results which replaced frustration in trying to go it alone.

Christ's heart for lost souls who return to Him is revealed in John 21:15-17,

> *So when they had eaten breakfast, Jesus said to Simon Peter, "Simon, son of Jonah, do you love Me more than these?" He said to Him, "Yes, Lord; You know that I love You." He said to him,* ***"Feed My lambs."*** (Emphasis mine)

'*Feeding the lambs*' refers to nurturing new believers who have been born again into the Kingdom of God. They need to be fed with 'pure milk' from the Lord. 1 Peter 2:2

(KJV) declares, *"as newborn babes, desire the pure milk of the word, that you may grow thereby."*

Next, Jesus asked Peter to feed His sheep (John 21:16):

He said to him again a second time, "Simon, son of Jonah, do you love Me?" He said to Him, "Yes, Lord; You know that I love You." He said to him, "Tend My sheep."

Who Owns the Sheep?

The 'sheep' are not the property of any human being; they belong to the Lord. He said, *"Feed my lambs"* and *"Feed my sheep"*. These statements referred to the many other disciples who were following Jesus apart from the twelve.

The sheep will always follow the shepherd who leads the way. This is the assignment Jesus instructed Peter to complete as a shepherd or pastor (v17).

Jesus continued, *"Simon, son of Jonah, do you love Me?"* Peter was grieved because Jesus asked him the third time, *"Do you love Me?"* Peter's final response: *"Lord, You know all things; You know that I love You."* Jesus then commissioned Peter, *"Feed My sheep."*

The final time Jesus says to Peter *feed my sheep*, He is guiding Peter on how to nurture new believers' faith in God. It is by teaching and guiding them so they will understand how to walk in the ways of the Lord.

The Shepherd's Role

1) **Take the sheep to drink water.** Jesus is described as the **Living Water**. He also said to the woman at the well that anyone who drinks of that water shall thirst again. However, those who drank of the Water of Life would never thirst again. (See John 4:13-14).

Jesus answered and said to her, "Whoever drinks of this water will thirst again, but whoever drinks of the water that I shall give him will never thirst. But the water that I shall give him will become in him a fountain of water springing up into everlasting life."

2) **Take the sheep to green pastures** as described in Psalm 23:2, *He makes me to lie down in green pastures; He leads me beside the still waters.* The colour **green** depicts new life, fruitfulness, abundance and provision. David relied on God as his Provider, Guide and Protector when he was tending his father's sheep.

3) **Guard us along the pathway.** Here again we embrace God's Divine Direction (Psalm 23:3) He restores my soul; He leads me in the paths of righteousness for His name's sake. Proverbs 3:5-6, *Trust in the Lord with all your heart, and lean not on your own understanding; In all your ways acknowledge Him, and He shall direct your paths.*

4) **Protect us so we fear no evil because the Lord is with us.** Psalm 23:4 reveals, *Yea, though I walk through the valley of the shadow of death, I will fear no evil; for*

You are with me; Your rod and Your staff, they comfort me. Psalm 91:9-12 further expounds the reward for those who make the LORD their hiding place: *Because you have made the Lord, who is my refuge, even the Most High, your dwelling place, No evil shall befall you, nor shall any plague come near your dwelling; For He shall give His angels charge over you, to keep you in all your ways. In their hands they shall bear you up, lest you dash your foot against a stone.*

A shepherd also has a rod of correction and the staff for protection and direction. When Jesus gave the parable of The Lost Sheep, He was explaining to the Pharisees and Scribes that *"This is My reason for coming into the world."* In other words, His purpose on earth was to minister to the tax collectors and sinners. Even if that only accounted for one percent of the population, it still mattered.

Before ascending to heaven, Jesus commissioned His disciples to preach the gospel to the whole world. By so doing He revealed God's main mission of redeeming and restoring lost souls back to Himself.

The Church

Jesus spoke about building the Church against which the gates of hell would not prevail. For many years many factors have caused the church to experience detachment and poor growth. These affect the church on an individual and organisational level, and as part of the body of Christ. Let us now examine four factors that negatively influence the Body of Christ today:

#1. Lack of Spiritual Hunger

The first factor is Lack of Spiritual Hunger for God and His Word. People end up leaving church because they lack interest in spiritual things or the Spirit of God. Tradition and culture play a major role in this area. The Church needs to be taught the Word of God step by step, teaching the Scriptures with sound doctrine that leads to maturity.

The leadership needs to nurture and ensure members' growth so that they can work with maturity within their ministry calling. As the Church grows in love its members will not become detached.

#2. Lack of Commitment

The growth that leads to results while preventing discouragement requires commitment. The expected growth is not automatic: process and patience are key elements. The Church also needs to be delivered from non-participation. Everyone is required to do their part; only then can the sheep be delivered from a prodigal state. The state of commitment will encourage everyone to develop a closer walk with God and have a sense of belonging.

#3. Lack of Connection

A major influence that causes people to backslide stems from lack of connection to God, His Word and the church's vison. Many believers are frustrated because they feel disconnected; this leads to lack of passion for spiritual matters.

The challenges every individual goes through has opened us up to experiencing daily miracles. Connection is known to ignite kindness between people where empowerment becomes a reality.

#4. Prodigal Prayers

Prayer should be the lifestyle of every child of God. The church that refuses to pray becomes easy prey to the enemy. Unfortunately, today many people talk of prayer but hardly pray. Many preach about prayer but hardly pray. Offering the service of prayer is a daily necessity for every child of God. Today prayer is being misunderstood as the means of getting *'things'* from God. Yet prayer was ultimately designed as an intimate means of communion between the child of God and Almighty God. Prayer is also what enhances the relationship between God and the church.

Time to Reflect:

Name three ways Jesus the Good Shepherd has been leading your life since you invited Him to be your guide.

Reflect on how much you really love Jesus.

Are you willing to give up time so that you will be able to spend more time serving your gifts to build the Kingdom of God?

Name one thing you will start doing to grow closer to God.

> Commit your way to the Lord, trust also in Him, and He shall bring it to pass.
> (Psalm 37:5)

Chapter Five:
The Lost and Found Parables

Let us now connect with three powerful parables Jesus used to illustrate the power of forgiveness and love. First, let us define what a PARABLE is.

The Merriam-Webster Dictionary describes a parable as:

a usually short fictitious story that illustrates a moral attitude or a religious principle for example the Biblical parable of the Good Samaritan.

something (such as a news story or a series of real events) likened to a parable in providing an instructive example or lesson.

Jesus Christ used simple relatable stories or parables to provide a more profound lesson. We can learn many amazing wisdom nuggets and everlasting truths from the divine wisdom of Jesus Christ by reflecting on the simple parables of the Bible.

The three parables we will unpack in this chapter are The Lost Sheep, The Lost Coin and The Lost Son. We briefly touched on The Lost Sheep in the previous chapter.

First, The Parable of The Lost Sheep

Luke 15:4-7 gives the account of Jesus' teaching on the parable of The Lost Sheep. The tax collectors and sinners moved closer to hear Jesus teach. The Pharisees and scribes were teachers of the Law who thought themselves superior to the multitude because of their high position in the Synagogue. They complained about the calibre of people who were eagerly waiting to listen to Jesus. This prompted Jesus to teach his listeners the following parable:

> *"What man of you, having a hundred sheep, if he loses one of them, does not leave the ninety-nine in the wilderness, and go after the one which is lost until he finds it? And when he has found it, he lays it on his shoulders, rejoicing. And when he comes home, he calls together his friends and neighbors, saying to them, '**Rejoice with me, for I have found my sheep which was lost!**' **I say to you that likewise there will be more joy in heaven over one sinner who repents than over ninety-nine just persons who need no repentance.***

Verses 6-7 portray the heart of God in joyfully receiving one lost sinner who asks Him for mercy. God is interested in every person on earth. He wants us all to be in right standing with the Father so that we will all enjoy an eternity of perpetual rejoicing in heaven.

The Pharisees were displeased with the people Jesus chose to spend time with, not realizing that the very purpose Jesus came to earth was to redeem the lost.

Do you know any church leaders who behave like the Pharisees and scribes? Do they try to stop the move of God in the church by segregating the 'lost sheep' from the 'found sheep'?

Jesus set us the perfect example of how to reach the lost and bring them to the knowledge of Christ. Everyone on earth needs to be given the opportunity to repent, turn from their wicked ways, and receive the gift of salvation.

Let us therefore seek God's righteousness through faith, as revealed in Romans 3:21-24:

> *But now the righteousness of God apart from the law is revealed, being witnessed by the Law and the Prophets, even the righteousness of God, through faith in Jesus Christ, to all and on all who believe. For there is no difference;* **for all have sinned and fall short of the glory of God, being justified freely by His grace through the redemption that is in Christ Jesus.**

Second, The Lost Coin

There is a lot we can learn from the Parable of The Lost Coin, recorded in Luke 15:8-10.

> *"Or what woman, having ten silver coins, if she loses one coin, does not light a lamp, sweep the house, and search carefully until she finds it? And when she has found it, she calls her friends and neighbors together, saying, 'Rejoice with me, for I have found the piece which I lost!' Likewise, I say to you,* **there is joy in the presence of the angels of God over one sinner who repents**.*"* (Emphasis mine)

Do you rejoice and celebrate when you find something you hold valuable? The LORD Jesus rejoices over one lost soul who is found after wandering around aimlessly.

Jesus shared the Parable of The Lost Coin with His disciples. This Parable holds significant value we can learn from and apply in our own lives. It is important to understand the order of events in finding and bringing those who are lost back into relationship with their Creator.

What happens when we can't find an item of great worth? We drop everything and go in search of it. The woman with the lost coin was no different. Here's her game plan.

- **Light the area**. Since the coin fell in a dark spot the woman must have lit a lamp to illuminate the ground around her.

- **Clean**. She then swept the floor to access the awkward corners that were hard to reach by hand.
- **Search**. Next, the woman would have embarked on an intentional search. The same is true of a believer who has lost their way and is trying to get back on track with serving the LORD.
- **Celebrate**. Once the woman found the lost coin, she called all her friends to celebrate. Likewise, when a sinner returns to God, they get to rejoice with other believers for finding the truth which sets them free.
- **Testify**. Call your friends and share your good news. Encourage them that the same fortune and blessings are available to all who keep the faith.

Pause and reflect on the following:

Where have we as individuals or as the Church gone wrong? How did we lose our direction?

Let us look within and reflect on how we can get back on track with what God has called us to do. Also consider why the path we took did not work so we can avoid taking a wrong turn again.

Third, The Lost Son

In the **_Parable of The Lost Son_**, the father split the inheritance equally between his two sons when the younger son asked to be released to go into the world in search of himself. Before long, the Prodigal Son's funds dwindled to the point where he ended up eating with the pigs. We know that pigs eat anything unclean or dirty; they are not particular about healthy dieting.

The son must have hit his lowest point in life before stopping to reflect on his current situation. He recalled that in his father's house, servants were treated much better than what he was experiencing in his desert season. Luke 15:11-32 records The Parable of the Lost Son. Let us reflect on the Prodigal Son's journey (v11-24)

> *Then He said: "A certain man had two sons. And the younger of them said to his father, 'Father, give me the portion of goods that falls to me.' So he divided to them his livelihood. And not many days after, the younger son gathered all together, journeyed to a far country, and there wasted his possessions with prodigal living. But when he had spent all, there arose a severe famine in that land, and he began to be in want. Then he went and joined himself to a citizen of that country, and he sent him into his fields to feed swine. And he would gladly have filled his stomach with the pods that the swine ate, and no one gave him anything.*

"But when he came to himself, he said, 'How many of my father's hired servants have bread enough and to spare, and I perish with hunger! I will arise and go to my father, and will say to him, "Father, I have sinned against heaven and before you, and I am no longer worthy to be called your son. Make me like one of your hired servants." ' "And he arose and came to his father. But when he was still a great way off, his father saw him and had compassion, and ran and fell on his neck and kissed him. ... "But the father said to his servants, *'Bring out the best robe and put it on him, and put a ring on his hand and sandals on his feet. And bring the fatted calf here and kill it, and let us eat and be merry; for this my son was dead and is alive again; he was lost and is found.' And they began to be merry.* (Emphasis mine)

When the wayward young man came to his senses, he was ready to be received as a servant, not wishing to presume upon his status as a son. He did not feel worthy of the title 'son'. However, his father lovingly received and even embraced him. He ordered the fattened calf to be slaughtered and prepared in a feast to celebrate his lost son's return.

The father's actions and words demonstrate enduring patience and expectant faith. This is symbolic of our Heavenly Father's commitment to love and receive all who come to Him in faith and humility. These are traits worth emulating in our own lives and ministries.

> *"Now his older son was in the field. And as he came and drew near to the house, he heard music and dancing. So he called one of the servants and asked what these things meant. And he said to him, 'Your brother has come, and because he has received him safe and sound, your father has killed the fatted calf.'* **"But he was angry and would not go in. Therefore his father came out and pleaded with him.** *So he answered and said to his father, 'Lo, these many years I have been serving you; I never transgressed your commandment at any time; and yet you never gave me a young goat, that I might make merry with my friends. But as soon as this son of yours came, who has devoured your livelihood with harlots, you killed the fatted calf for him.' (v25-30)* (Emphasis mine)

Sometimes jealousy gets in the way of sound reasoning. The older son did not understand the father's point of rejoicing over one *'lost and found'*. He became angry and would not receive his long-lost brother who had made an intelligent and brave decision to return home, amid certain criticism and judgment from others who knew his story. Read the father's response to his eldest son:

> **"And he said to him, 'Son, you are always with me, and all that I have is yours. It was**

right that we should make merry and be glad, for your brother was dead and is alive again, and was lost and is found.' " (Emphasis mine)

The wise father patiently explained to the hurting older son that everything they owned belonged to him (v31-32). It is notable that the father did not chastise the son in anger. After all, as Proverbs 15:1 reminds us, *A gentle answer turns away wrath.*

Time to Reflect:

Pause for a moment and consider:

1. Are you where God wants you to be in the ministry?

2. Are you serving your gifts fully?

If you are not fully aligned with God's will you need to reflect on what He has impressed on your heart about your calling and purpose.

3. Are you struggling with past hurts from being let down or disappointed by others? Do you have any regrets? Release the hurt and regrets and ask God to heal you as you forgive yourself.

4. Choose to return to your Creator and ask Him to direct your path so that you will be fruitful where you are planted.

> And it shall come to pass in the last days, says God, that I will pour out of My Spirit on all flesh; your sons and your daughters shall prophesy, your young men shall see visions, your old men shall dream dreams.
>
> (Acts 2:17)

Chapter Six:
The Promise to the Church

Before the early church, we saw how our fathers were religious. Once instruction proceeded through a priest, the children of Israel adhered to it without checking whether it was convenient for them or not. Even today we have people like David who understood God as a Loving Father while others followed their religious acts. The Bible teaches us that David and his troop went into the temple when they were hungry and ate of the bread within.

When we look at various men and women described in the Bible, we see God's character exhibited and admire the personality of those who walked in His footsteps. Otherwise, we would not have people named after great men and women mentioned in the Bible. For example, we name our children *Samuel* because he listened to God, *Esther* because of her God-fearing attributes, *David* a man after God's heart, *Sarah* a mother of nations, and many more.

Ask yourself, *"At the end of my work on earth, will Heaven be proud of me?" "Is my name inscribed in Heaven?"* Some names fade away when the owners leave this earth while others remain in the hearts of men. If you are not living your God-ordained purpose on earth, are you not behaving like a Prodigal son or daughter?

I have often wondered if this has been the way Christianity has been handled over the years. Curiously, I believe the great Generals would not have been recorded in the template of people's hearts if all they were after was ephemeral or short-lived.

More recently, knowledge has increased, and many now hold on to the chapters of Scripture that justify their sinful acts without any consideration on what they are to do about it. Nowadays, many see themselves as having been called without any form of responsibility. There is no distinct difference between the world and the believers these days. We believe that God sees the heart and not what we wear. I wonder how we got here; indeed, the Scriptures are being fulfilled in our day.

Beloved, choose wisely the Scriptures you wish God to fulfil in your life. The Bible says in Acts 2:17, *"In the last days, God will pour out His Spirit upon all flesh."* The Scriptures continue, *"In the last day, some will depart from the word of Truth, men becoming lovers of themselves, and the love of many will wax cold"* (2 Timothy 3). Let us therefore be careful about what we choose and create a good testimony for others to emulate, knowing that our children are watching us.

Before we proceed, let us reflect on how many believers think for God and still murmur to Him, trying to cover up their shortcomings. Follow closely what Proverbs 3:5-6 says, "*Trust in the LORD with all thine heart; and lean not unto thine own understanding. In all thy ways acknowledge him, and he shall direct thy paths."* (KJV)

Pause for a few minutes and consider what you have done since you started following Christ.

Have you seen someone trying to force things to happen on their terms? One might be saying they can overcome certain challenges when it is clearly not possible without God's intervention. When their plan fails, some people blame God. Is this fair as a believer?

God is not our equal. He is compassionate, loving and forgiving. Yet when we fail to ask for His direction and timing in our plans, we can only blame ourselves if the plan fails to yield the expected fruit.

Let us read the following verses from Proverbs 3:7-8 (KJV) slowly. *"Be not wise in thine own eyes: fear the LORD and depart from evil. It shall be health to thy navel, and marrow to thy bones."*

Are you not smart in your own way? Permit me to say this, you can be successful but not according to God's standards. If God has not ordained your success, it will inevitably end on earth without an eternal reward.

The Bible says, *"...on this rock will I build my Church and the gates of hell shall not prevail"* (Matthew 16:18). Many promises are targeted at the end times, meanwhile many Christians are sleeping. Are we not prodigal? Consider a believer who feels the urge to not go to church, and gives excuses such as "*God is everywhere*," is that not a prodigal?

What about a believer who is in competition to amass earthly possessions just to show proof that God answers prayer, are they not displaying prodigal tendencies? This is a crucial and pertinent time to know why we are living today.

That prodigal brother (or Church) decided to go back to his father's house expecting no reward. Be aware that not everyone will have a second chance. We are God's 'building' because God's Spirit lives in us. He that lives in us knows all about us because He is very present. We can never lie to Him since He is always there. Are we seeking after He who can kill the flesh and the soul rather than looking inward to see the need to return to God?

Various promises are being fulfilled in our lifetime and the Word of God cannot return to Him void. We must therefore rest on His unfailing Word as Revelation 3 explains. Neither money nor earthly wealth can ever justify a man. Only those who have spiritual ears can hear what the Spirit of God is saying to us, since the Church will be justified before the Lord.

Put another way, we cannot serve both God and money because God knows that a time is coming when people will chase after money and their hearts will be blinded to spiritual things.

We will not account to any man on the day of reckoning; not even the pastor will vouch for you. Therefore, let us be the epistle people will read. Let us return to the LORD for He is coming soon. Be careful not to lose your post for an earthly race my friend. Instead, focus on pleasing God for the time is much closer than we realize.

In the world today everyone is aspiring to be established. They fail to realise that the only establishment that can stand forever is the one made for the purpose of the Gospel. Everyone is now minding their business; very few are demonstrating any compassion or empathy. Do yourself a favour:

It is time to change!!!

Reflect on the following Scriptures:

"In the last day, some will depart from the word of Truth, men becoming lovers of themselves, and the love of many will wax cold" (2 Timothy 3:1).

But he who endures to the end shall be saved. And this gospel of the kingdom will be preached in all the world as a witness to all the nations, and then the end will come. (Matthew 24:12-14)

Pray and ask the Holy Spirit to help you endure in your Christian walk.

Commit to listening to the Holy Spirit and allow Him to daily guide your path so that you will endure to the end.

> But he who endures to the end shall be saved. And this gospel of the kingdom will be preached in all the world as a witness to all the nations, and then the end will come.
>
> (Matthew 24:14)

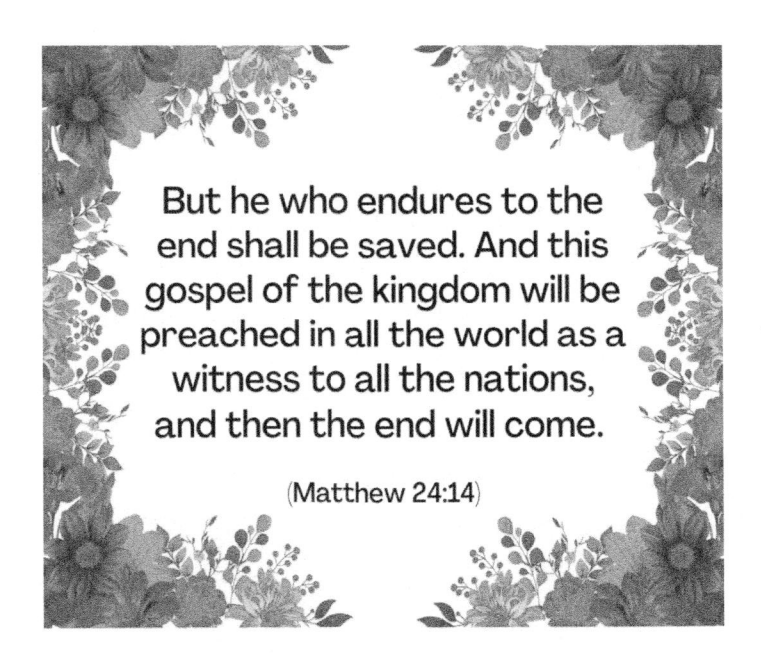

Chapter Seven:
Misplaced Priority

The Prodigal Church birthed misplaced priority. Let us examine Revelation 1 verse 6 which reveals: *"and has made us kings and priests to His God and Father, to Him be glory and dominion forever and ever. Amen."*

Did you notice who God says we are? He calls us **kings** and **priests**! He did not say that we would be made kings and priests. *We already are!* We are reading the present-day ministry of Christ. Reality comes by faith in the Word.

I once preached on the topic, *"Church, where are you?"* (Genesis 3:9). Are you in the right place where God expects you to be? To some, once there is a credit alert, their soul leaps for joy whenever they gather with the brethren.

Let us talk about you: what is the source of your joy? Ponder this as we journey through. Read Ephesians 1:22-23 closely:

> *"And He put all things under His feet, and gave Him to be head over all things to the church, which is His body, the fullness of Him who fills all in all."*

The Bible made it clear that Jesus Christ committed all the power to the Church. We are the glorious church.

1 Corinthians 3:9 (KJV) further clarifies our position within the Body of Christ: *"For we are labourers together with God: ye are God's husbandry, ye are God's building."*

This is our reality in Christ Jesus. We are not to be slaves to false gods; the Almighty God Himself called us and made us co-labourers with Him.

Apostle Paul outlined his calling in God's overall plan in 1 Corinthians 3:10:

> *"According to the grace of God which is given unto me, as a wise masterbuilder, I have laid the foundation, and another buildeth thereon. But let every man take heed how he buildeth thereupon."*

Paul spoke the following words based on the measure of faith he had which was birthed from an inner conviction.

> *"For I am persuaded, that neither death, nor life, nor angels, nor principalities, nor powers, nor things present, nor things to come, nor height, nor depth, nor any other creature, shall be able to separate us from the love of God, which is in Christ Jesus our Lord." (Romans 8:38-39)*

Paul declared that not even life, angels or any other reason could separate him from the love of God. Many people today seek after angelic ministration. However, what is separating Christians nowadays is not life or angels; those things are not recorded in this chapter.

Let me ask you: "*Do you know why you are on earth?*" It is to fulfil God's eternal agenda here on earth.

Are you contradicting God's purpose for your life by focusing on what He has not called you to? If you answered, 'yes' or 'I'm not sure', it is time for you to make a choice.

1 Corinthians 3:11 confirms: "*For no other foundation can anyone lay than that which is laid, which is Jesus Christ.*" Christ is the foundation of our reality; however, the foundation you lay on Him matters.

The above evidence has shown us that the word "*prodigal*" is not farfetched, it is happening already due to "MISPLACEMENT OF PRIORITY".

Time to Reflect:

1. Ask God to speak to you in the silence. Allow Him to gently guide you to what He has called you to accomplish on earth.

2. Write down what God reveals to you.

3. Finally, create a strategy to get back on track and daily ask the Holy Spirit to guide your decisions and equip you for your assignment.

Let everything that has breath praise the Lord.

(Psalm 150:6)

Chapter Eight:
Prodigal Praise and Worship

Our bodies are instruments of praise to the Lord. The Bible declares, *"Let everything that has breath praise the Lord."* (Psalm 150:6) Praise is the vehicle by which God connects with His beloved children as we worship Him wholeheartedly.

We need three things to unlock godly praise and worship:

#1. The Lord will work with us when we are humble in heart.

#2. The Lord will only work with vessels of honour.

#3. God is looking for people who will worship Him in Spirit and truth.

Firstly, when we humble ourselves, we allow God's power and glory to shine through our worship. We decrease so that His Holy Spirit may increase and manifest through us.

Next, we need to purify our hearts before the Lord so that what we present before Him is a holy, honorable and acceptable sacrifice of praise before our Creator. The very breath we use to praise our Heavenly Father comes from Him. When God breathed His breath of life into the first man Adam, man became a living being.

Thirdly, we can only worship God in Spirit and truth when our hearts are right before Him. Otherwise, we are likened to a noisy gong or a clanging cymbal if we have not confessed our sin and humanity before Him in an act of reverence and humility (1 Corinthians 13). Confessing our sins before God and asking Him to purify our hearts will enable every true worshipper to connect with the heart of God. Only then will our praise and worship be acceptable before our Creator as a sweet fragrance because God dwells in the praises of His beloved children.

These are the characteristics of the true worshipper who is enabled to draw the congregation before the Lord in communal praise and worship.

What is worship?

The Merriam-Webster dictionary employs two main verb forms to describe 'worship': transitive and intransitive.

As a transitive verb **worship** means:

1: to honor or show reverence for as a divine being or supernatural power

2: to regard with great or extravagant respect, honor, or devotion

For example: *A celebrity worshipped by her fans.*

As an intransitive verb: *to perform or take part in worship or an act of worship*

Worship as a noun refers to

1: reverence offered a divine being or supernatural power also an act of expressing such reverence.

2: a form of religious practice with its creed and ritual.

3: extravagant respect or admiration for or devotion to an object of esteem

One can also refer to 'worship of the dollar':

4 chiefly British: a person of importance —used as a title for various officials (such as magistrates and some mayors)

It is amazing how over the years worship within the church setting has turned into an enterprise where people are using their gifts to earn an income. Let us compare the praise and worship in churches in the 1970s-1980s to the 2020s scenario. The millennium brought New Age thinking and secular practices which covertly filtered into the church. Meanwhile, many leaders' eyes appear to be dimmed by these ungodly practices, while others simply ignore its existence.

While in previous generations we used to sing and clap our hands to praise the Lord, many musicians in today's world will not lead worship unless they are paid for their services. Every worshipper should have a place where they worship, and everyone needs to be spiritually fed. Philippians 4:4-9 declares,

> *"Rejoice in the Lord always. Again I will say, rejoice!" Let your gentleness (graciousness,*

forbearance) be known to all men. The Lord is at hand. Be anxious for nothing, but in everything by prayer and supplication, with thanksgiving, let your requests be made known to God; and the peace of God, which surpasses all understanding, will guard your hearts and minds through Christ Jesus. Finally, brethren, whatever things are true, whatever things are noble, whatever things are just, whatever things are pure, whatever things are lovely, **whatever things are of good report, if there is any virtue and if there is anything praiseworthy— meditate on these things.** *The things which you learned and received and heard and saw in me, these do, and the God of peace will be with you.*

Paul instructs us on gaining a heart of true worship and reverence to Almighty God who is the only One we should adore. He remains faithful to supply all our needs.

Note that the above scenario should not be confused with a church paying the musician who is training the team in godly worship and excellence. For example, some prolific musicians in churches offer weekly choral practice as a service aside from leading Sunday worship.

Unfortunately, some worshippers stop respecting their pastors after they are elevated to the position of leading praise and worship. Such brethren forget it is the Lord who has lifted and bestowed honour upon them. With honour comes responsibility, but when it is abused the worshipper risks facing God's wrath.

Accountability is essential in every ministry calling. If one is unable to attend a rehearsal or service, they should let the leadership know in advance. Doing so ensures that one is observing due protocol and displaying good manners.

The same applies to preachers, elders and ministers who are called to minister elsewhere. Let your team leader know in case something happens, otherwise, if you ran into trouble, who would you call for help? The church leadership where you previously served and left without warning might not be inclined to readily step in and bail you out. *Why not*? They may not feel it their responsibility since you chose not to confide your movements with them.

Everyone should have a spiritual home where they are protected and accountable. Just as we all have a physical address where we return at the end of the day's activities, our spiritual grounding and home are also necessary.

Many worshippers globally have become a name tag or brand. They are more interested in attaining fame than having an excellent spirit to worship the Lord in Spirit and in truth. When you watch the media, do you notice how many worshippers and preachers have shifted their focus to raising money rather than making an altar call? We need to return to our roots of true worship as we reverence God and incur His favour as vessels of honour.

Other forms of worship we can empower within the body of Christ include charity work, evangelism, and various outreach programs. Within the church we can grow our worship through youth programs, children's ministry, men's and women's fellowship, hospitality and more. All in all, our focus should always be to ***honour the LORD with our spiritual gift of worship and adoration for Who He Is***, rather than what He can do for us.

Commit to serving God with a grateful heart wherever He has planted you as you grow in your ministry gifting. Reflect on the following areas as you consider how you will empower your true act of worship going forward.

Time to Reflect:

Consider your form of worship:

1. Are you glorifying God your Creator, or are you performing a service aimed at receiving earthly accolades from mere mortals?

2. How will you draw closer to God in a true act of worship?

What gifts will you employ in your true act of worship to God for His faithfulness and holiness?

(Consider: music, other acts of service within the church, outreach programs, changing your focus and expectations as you choose to joyfully serve the Lord with gladness). Record your thoughts below.

> And Jacob said to his household and to all who were with him, "Put away the foreign gods that are among you, purify yourselves, and change your garments."
>
> (Genesis 35:2)

Chapter Nine:
Change into Garments of Honour

When the Lord cleanses us, He gives us the garments of salvation. Jacob instructed his people to cleanse themselves and put on new garments before they presented themselves before the Lord. A Holy God requires holy and pure hearts, minds and bodies so that He will receive our sacrifices and petitions.

Read Jacob's Return to Bethel in Genesis 35:1-3, 5-7:

> *Then God said to Jacob, "Arise, go up to Bethel and dwell there; and make an altar there to God, who appeared to you when you fled from the face of Esau your brother." And Jacob said to his household and to all who were with him,* ***"Put away the foreign gods that are among you, purify yourselves, and change your garments.*** *Then let us arise and go up to Bethel; and I will make an altar there to God, who answered me in the day of my distress and has been with me in the way which I have gone."*
> *...And they journeyed, and the terror of God was upon the cities that were all around them, and they did not pursue the sons of Jacob. So Jacob came to Luz (that is, Bethel), which is in the land of Canaan, he and all the people who were with*

him. **And he built an altar there and called the place El Bethel, because there God appeared to him when he fled from the face of his brother.** (Emphasis mine)

After this encounter, God changed Jacob's name to Israel and made a covenant to bless him and his descendants forever (v9-14).

> **Then God appeared to Jacob again**, when he came from Padan Aram, **and blessed him**. And God said to him, "Your name is Jacob; your name shall not be called Jacob anymore, but Israel shall be your name." So **He called his name Israel.** Also **God said to him: "I am God Almighty. Be fruitful and multiply; a nation and a company of nations shall proceed from you, and kings shall come from your body. The land which I gave Abraham and Isaac I give to you; and to your descendants after you I give this land."** Then God went up from him in the place where He talked with him. **So Jacob set up a pillar in the place where He talked with him, a pillar of stone; and he poured a drink offering on it, and he poured oil on it.** (Emphasis mine)

There is an everlasting blessing attached to our obedience to heed God's Voice. When we shed off our old filthy garments of the old self, old attitudes and thoughts, old actions and negative words, God works for us and through us because we are now His vessels of honour. The Spirit of God can only operate within a clean vessel, which is our purified hearts.

Another form of exchanging garments is seen in the story of Joseph's life (read Genesis 37-39).

Jacob, being very fond of his son Joseph, created a special multicoloured garment for him which represented his son's multi-talented character and gifts. However, this created a division between Joseph's older brothers who plotted to get rid of him. Afterwards, when Joseph went to check on his brothers, (Gen. 37:23) they grabbed him and threw him into a pit and deceived their father that Joseph had been mauled by wild animals. They dipped the garment in goat's blood and showed it to their father. The brothers later sold Joseph to slave traders, and he ended up in Egypt. (v31-35). The brothers' deception caused deep grief to their father.

Joseph then found favour with Potiphar, the prison keeper, who gave him a garment. Shortly after, Potiphar's wife ripped off the garment from Joseph's body when she tried to seduce him, and he rejected her advances. When she lied about Joseph he was thrown in prison where he languished for two years. While there, Josephs gifts of interpreting dreams were sharpened; this became the steppingstone to his release and uplifting when Pharaoh needed someone to interpret his unusual dreams.

God gives His children many garments. The greatest garment Joseph received was the LORD's salvation.

When he was sold to Potiphar, he received the garment of salvation; later when Joseph was released from the prison dungeon, he received the garments of favour and recognition.

Psalm 91:14-16 states,

> *"Because he has set his love upon Me, therefore I will deliver him; I will set him on high, because he has known My name. 15 He shall call upon Me, and I will answer him; I will be with him in trouble; I will deliver him and honor him. 16 With long life I will satisfy him, and show him My salvation."*

Have you read the story of how Jesus healed a blind man called Bartimaeus, recorded in Mark 10:46-52?

> *Now they came to Jericho. As He went out of Jericho with His disciples and a great multitude, blind Bartimaeus, the son of Timaeus, sat by the road begging. And when he heard that it was Jesus of Nazareth, he began to cry out and say,* **"Jesus, Son of David, have mercy on me!"** *Then many warned him to be quiet; but he cried out all the more, "Son of David, have mercy on me!"* **So Jesus stood still and commanded him to be called.** *Then they called the blind man, saying to him, "Be of good cheer. Rise, He is calling you."* **And throwing aside his garment, he rose and came to Jesus.** *So Jesus answered and said to him,* **"What do you**

want Me to do for you?" *The blind man said to Him, "Rabboni, that I may receive my sight."* **Then Jesus said to him, "Go your way; your faith has made you well."** *And immediately he received his sight and followed Jesus on the road.*

When the blind man heard that Jesus was passing by, he called out to Him, seeking to get His attention. When the crowd tried to discourage him from calling Jesus, Bartimaeus called louder. His efforts were rewarded when Jesus asked him, "**What do you want Me to do for you?**" The blind man replied, "*I want to be made whole.*" The same response is available to us when we call on the Name of Jesus.

There is a blessing attached to obediently shedding our old garments. Blind Bartimaeus received new physical sight, and a renewed heart of deeper faith in the God he called upon.

Believers in Christ sometimes go into worldly members' camps, disrobe them from their spiritual garments and take on an unbeliever's clothing. For example, some people go to sorcerers and fortune tellers seeking answers for life's challenges. Followers of Christ should not look elsewhere for answers as it dilutes one's faith and total reliance on God Almighty who is able to do all things when we call on Him.

When Jesus went to Lazarus' grave, He groaned in prayer as those surrounding Him wondered, *What is He going to do now*? Let us read the account of Jesus and death, the last enemy (John 11:28-44):

And when she (Martha) had said these things, she went her way and secretly called Mary her sister, saying, "The Teacher has come and is calling for you." As soon as she heard that, she arose quickly and came to Him. ... Then, when Mary came where Jesus was, and saw Him, she fell down at His feet, saying to Him, "Lord, if You had been here, my brother would not have died." Therefore, when Jesus saw her weeping, and the Jews who came with her weeping, He groaned in the spirit and was troubled. And He said, "Where have you laid him?" They said to Him, "Lord, come and see." **Jesus wept.** *Then the Jews said, "See how He loved him!" And some of them said, "Could not this Man, who opened the eyes of the blind, also have kept this man from dying?"*

Jesus, concerned about growing the people's faith, would not leave their friend Lazarus in the grave. He prayed to His Father and a miracle happened before those present.

Then Jesus, again groaning in Himself, came to the tomb. *It was a cave, and a stone lay against it. Jesus said,* **"Take away the stone."**...

Jesus said to her, "Did I not say to you that if you would believe you would see the glory of God?"

Then they took away the stone from the place where the dead man was lying. ***And Jesus lifted up His eyes and said, "Father, I thank You that You have heard Me. And I know that You always hear Me, but because of the people who are standing by I said this, that they may believe that You sent Me."*** *Now when He had said these things, He cried with a loud voice,* ***"Lazarus, come forth!"*** *And he who had died came out bound hand and foot with graveclothes, and his face was wrapped with a cloth.* ***Jesus said to them, "Loose him, and let him go."*** (Emphasis mine)

Jesus gave the command to remove the wraps covering Lazarus's body and let him go. New life was literally restored to Jesus' friend who had been dead in the tomb for four days. Imagine how amazed the crowd, and especially Lazarus's sisters were, to see their brother and friend restored to life!

At the Name of Jesus miracles happen for everyone who believes in His Power and unfailing Word. Try Him today and see what He will do for you, my friend.

Time to Reflect:

In what areas do you need to restore your garments of honour?

If you saw a prodigal son or daughter drifting from the ways of the Lord, how would you encourage them to return to the fold?

Chapter Ten:
Heeding God's Voice

God revels His plans to Elijah

1 Kings 19 records how prophet Elijah escaped from the wicked queen Jezebel. After Elijah executed all the false prophets, King Ahab relayed the news to his wife Jezebel. This displeased her greatly and she vowed to retaliate (v2). A distraught Elijah fled into the wilderness and sat under a broom tree, totally broken, saying, (v4) *"It is enough! Now, Lord, take my life, for I am no better than my fathers!"*

As Elijah slept, an angel of the Lord appeared to him twice and provided food and water to renew his physical strength (v5-8). Thereafter Elijah fasted and travelled to the mountain of God named Horeb for forty days and forty nights. The ministration signified that God was with him.

Then the Word of the Lord met him as he hid in a cave in the mountain, asking (v9-10),

> *"What are you doing here, Elijah?" So he said, "I have been very zealous for the Lord God of hosts; for the children of Israel have forsaken Your covenant, torn down Your altars, and killed*

Your prophets with the sword. I alone am left; and they seek to take my life."

Can you distinguish the Voice of the Lord when He is calling you to serve His purpose? In 1 Kings 19:11-14 we learn that the Voice of the Lord can manifest in different ways. Elijah identified and reacted to the Voice of God.

Then He said, "Go out, and stand on the mountain before the Lord." And behold, the Lord passed by, and a great and strong wind tore into the mountains and broke the rocks in pieces before the Lord, but the Lord was not in the wind; and after the wind an earthquake, but the Lord was not in the earthquake; and after the earthquake a fire, but the Lord was not in the fire; and after the fire a still small voice. So it was, when Elijah heard it, that he wrapped his face in his mantle and went out and stood in the entrance of the cave. Suddenly a voice came to him, and said, "What are you doing here, Elijah?" And he said, "I have been very zealous for the Lord God of hosts; because the children of Israel have forsaken Your covenant, torn down Your altars, and killed Your prophets with the sword. I alone am left; and they seek to take my life."

When God calls us, He has a definite assignment for us to fulfil. Time is of the essence if we are to fulfil God's Divine purpose in what He has designed for us. Elijah was obedient to follow the Lord's instruction to anoint

Hazael and Jehu as kings, and Elisha as the prophet who would succeed him (v15-16).

God also prepares His prophets to step into their calling, as revealed in Elisha's quick response (v19-21):

> *So he departed from there, and found Elisha the son of Shaphat, who was plowing with twelve yoke of oxen before him, and he was with the twelfth. Then Elijah passed by him and threw his mantle on him. And he left the oxen and ran after Elijah, and said, "Please let me kiss my father and my mother, and then I will follow you." And he said to him, "Go back again, for what have I done to you?" So Elisha turned back from him, and took a yoke of oxen and slaughtered them and boiled their flesh, using the oxen's equipment, and gave it to the people, and they ate. Then he arose and followed Elijah, and became his servant.*

Consider what assignment God has called you to fulfil. If you have been jealous for the Lord, do not worry about who else is completing their mission. Stay in your lane and follow what the Lord says to you. Remember, He will back you up and provide the resources you need for the assignment.

Do not depart from God's glory

What happens when we step out of position with God's calling upon our lives? Let us examine a few examples and note the lessons learned from each scenario.

1 Samuel 28:1-25 records Saul consulting a medium after he was intimidated by the great Philistine army. Saul had sinned against God by not following His instructions. As a result, the glory of the Lord had departed from Saul. When he enquired before the Lord concerning the Philistine army, there was no answer. Saul then resorted to taking drastic measures. He called a female spiritist to bring up Samuel so he could enquire from the prophet of God. (Saul had already put out all the spiritists and mediums from the land.) God's glory now rested upon David who would soon succeed Saul as king over Israel.

> *Now it happened in those days that the Philistines gathered their armies together for war, to fight with Israel. And Achish said to David, "You assuredly know that you will go out with me to battle, you and your men." So David said to Achish, "Surely you know what your servant can do." And Achish said to David, "Therefore I will make you one of my chief guardians forever."*

> *Now Samuel had died, and all Israel had lamented for him and buried him in Ramah, in his own city. ... When Saul saw the army of the Philistines, he was afraid, and his heart trembled greatly. And when Saul inquired of the Lord, the Lord did not answer him, either by dreams or by Urim or by the prophets. ... And Saul perceived that it was Samuel, and he stooped with his face to the ground and bowed down. Now Samuel said to Saul, "Why have you disturbed me by*

bringing me up?" And Saul answered, "I am deeply distressed; for the Philistines make war against me, and God has departed from me and does not answer me anymore, neither by prophets nor by dreams. Therefore I have called you, that you may reveal to me what I should do." Then Samuel said: "So why do you ask me, seeing the Lord has departed from you and has become your enemy? And the Lord has done for Himself as He spoke by me. For the Lord has torn the kingdom out of your hand and given it to your neighbor, David. Because you did not obey the voice of the Lord nor execute His fierce wrath upon Amalek, therefore the Lord has done this thing to you this day. Moreover the Lord will also deliver Israel with you into the hand of the Philistines. And tomorrow you and your sons will be with me. The Lord will also deliver the army of Israel into the hand of the Philistines."

The woman then prepared a meal for Saul for he had fasted day and night. When his strength was renewed, Saul and his friends went on their way.

What a loving God we serve! He gives second chances when we make a mistake. *Why*? Because He knows we are human. We feel fear, have doubts, and are constantly faced with human emotions that sometimes cause us to sin by not responding to what God is instructing us to do.

Quick word of caution: Choose to go forward; do not open any window for the enemy to come in and derail your mission. Do not play with the Holy Spirit. Choose to do what is right in the face of adversity and deep testing.

When David had the opportunity to avenge himself for his master's cruel treatment, he refused to hurt the Lord's anointed. 1 Samuel 24:8-12 records David's honourable action when he had the opportunity to retaliate when King Saul was pursuing him with the intention to kill him.

> *David also arose afterward, went out of the cave, and called out to Saul, saying, "My lord the king!" And when Saul looked behind him, David stooped with his face to the earth, and bowed down. And David said to Saul: "Why do you listen to the words of men who say, 'Indeed David seeks your harm'? Look, this day your eyes have seen that the Lord delivered you today into my hand in the cave, and someone urged me to kill you. But my eye spared you, and I said,* **'I will not stretch out my hand against my lord, for he is the Lord's anointed.'** *Moreover, my father, see! Yes, see the corner of your robe in my hand! For in that I cut off the corner of your robe, and did not kill you, know and see that there is neither evil nor rebellion in my hand, and I have not sinned against you. Yet you hunt my life to take it. Let the Lord judge between you and me, and let the Lord avenge*

me on you. But my hand shall not be against you.

Saul was busy chasing David, intending to kill him because of jealousy. Saul should have repented before the Lord for his sins and evil acts against the Lord's anointed servant David.

Samson was a man with a clear purpose. Sometimes we get into a deep sleep until our glory is taken from us. Samson's hair represented his glory.

David fell into sin because he was out of position at a time of war. He stayed home and lusted after another man's wife. After sinning with her, David killed her husband when he discovered she was pregnant with his child. God in His lovingkindness declared concerning king David: *"But my mercy shall not depart away from him, as I took it from Saul, whom I removed from before you."* (2 Samuel 7:15) When we make a wrong turn God is merciful to redeem and restore His anointed and chosen children.

Have you heard the story of the two Old Testament women who each gave birth to a baby boy? The first mother fell asleep. When she later awoke, she was mortified to discover that the baby lying on her bosom was not hers. After the second woman's baby died in the night, the mother cunningly switched him with the sleeping mother's living baby. Eventually the matter was brought before king Solomon who unraveled the mystery and restored the living baby to his birth mother. You can read the account of Solomon's wise judgment in 1 Kings 3:16-28.

What happens when believers are asleep? Thieves come and steal their inheritance. Do not let your Divine inheritance and assignment be taken away from you when you are spiritually asleep. You cannot discern the things of God when you are spiritually asleep. Always be alert and on your guard lest the enemy visits and takes what is yours.

1 Peter 5:8 warns us to *Be sober, be vigilant; because your adversary the devil walks about like a roaring lion, seeking whom he may devour*. If we lack spiritual discernment and alertness, we will miss out on accessing every blessing the Lord has made available to us.

In Matthew 13:24-30 we read the Parable of the wheat and the tares.

> *...The kingdom of heaven is like a man who sowed good seed in his field; but while men slept, his enemy came and sowed tares among the wheat and went his way. But when the grain had sprouted and produced a crop, then the tares also appeared. So the servants of the owner came and said to him, 'Sir, did you not sow good seed in your field? How then does it have tares?'* **He said to them, 'An enemy has done this.'** *The servants said to him, 'Do you want us then to go and gather them up?' But he said, 'No, lest while you gather up the tares you*

also uproot the wheat with them. Let both grow together until the harvest, and at the time of harvest I will say to the reapers, "First gather together the tares and bind them in bundles to burn them, but gather the wheat into my barn." ' "

Be on your guard and at the appointed time the Lord will separate the lies from the truth and grant you what is yours.

Sometimes your enemy will taunt and ridicule you to make you fear. 1 Samuel 17 gives an account of a Philistine named Goliath who taunted the Israelites. The giant showed off his strength and dared any Israelite to fight him. Saul and his entire army were greatly terrified, fearing for their lives, as recorded in verse 11: *When Saul and all Israel heard these words of the Philistine, they were dismayed and greatly afraid.*

David arrived bringing food for his brothers who were part of the army. After seeing the army's fear and hearing the giant's boast, he enquired what reward the one who conquered the Philistine would receive (v26-27):

Then David spoke to the men who stood by him, saying, "What shall be done for the man who kills this Philistine and takes away the reproach from Israel? For who is this uncircumcised Philistine, that he should defy the armies of the living God?" And the people answered him in this manner, saying, "So shall it be done for the man who kills him."

The story concludes with David defeating Goliath with only five pebbles and a sling. All Israel rejoiced and were saved from certain destruction. God fought for them through His servant David who the prophet Samuel had secretly anointed when he visited David's father Jesse's home.

Whenever we face any trouble, we can confidently call on the Lord who fights for us and grants us the victory against our enemies. Luke 19:41-44 gives an account of Jesus weeping over Jerusalem.

Now as He drew near, He saw the city and wept over it, saying, "If you had known, even you, especially in this your day, the things that make for your peace! But now they are hidden from your eyes. For days will come upon you when your enemies will build an embankment around you, surround you and close you in on every side, and level you, and your children within you, to the ground; and they will not leave in you one stone upon another, because you did not know the time of your visitation."

Every prodigal son or daughter who wants to be restored to the fold needs to search the Word of God and discover where we went wrong. When we repent and turn from our wicked ways we will be reunited and be in right standing with our Redeemer who will guide us in His righteous paths. God only works with willing hearts. Jesus came to redeem the lost and restore them back to Himself.

Time to Reflect:

As you examine your life, consider where you are not satisfied and what needs to change.

In what areas do you need to restore your garments of honour?

May the LORD reveal His plan and purpose for your life as you walk in your newness and wholeness in spirit and in truth in Jesus' Mighty Name.

> Behold what manner of love the Father has bestowed on us, that we should be called children of God! Therefore the world does not know us, because it did not know Him.
>
> (1 John 3:1)

Chapter Eleven:
How Can We Return to the Father?

The prodigal son came back to his senses and reasoned with himself. In the same manner, we need to go back to the Lord, repent and follow the true path. We should light our lamps and sweep out whatever is unclean. Once we are back on track, we should voice our joy to let others know we have found 'the lost coin'. Share the news that we have returned to the fold of the other ninety-nine sheep who kept the faith and those who kept their lamps burning.

Let us all rethink and reason using the Word of God as our guide so that no one else will deceive us again. Our light should shine bright so that we will not be swayed away from the Truth with false doctrines.

Even the very elect will be deceived; may our names not be among those deceived (Matthew 24:24). Some people meet men and women who are not walking in the path of the Kingdom of God. This is the reason why some men do not enjoy the benefits and blessings of a believer.

For the Church to be restored back we must have a right heart before the Lord and maintain it so that we may enjoy the benefits of a believer. Many believers have knowledge but lack understanding of how to properly apply it.

It is possible to have knowledge with no understanding. Proverbs 1:5 declares that wisdom grants you information or learning but understanding allows you to process the information and to convert it to wealth. If we do not return to God, we will cause confusion and pain to other believers. Furthermore, many who are watching us and those who come after us will not admire us nor be inspired by our leadership.

God called you as a believer with an assignment. Similarly, God chose Joshua for an assignment and not Caleb. God called Moses and not Aaron. God looks at one's heart rather than their age. Aaron had his own calling before God. David was qualified among his brothers when Samuel went to anoint a king from among Jesse's sons, as 1 Samuel 16:7 reveals.

We all need to be accountable and responsible. Paul was gifted with the ability to rebuke and encourage others. As a result, many people looked up to him. Timothy learned a great deal from Paul. On the other hand, Barnabas could be counted upon to tell the truth about what someone was doing wrong.

Consider*: Who can correct you whenever you go wrong? Who tells you the truth and doesn't paint you white whenever you make a mistake?*

Scripture gives us many examples of people who displayed various strengths as well as those with shortcomings. For example, 2 Samuel 13:3 records how Amnon had a bad advisor named Jonadab; this association later caused Amnon's death. For two years Absalom quietly nursed malice against Amnon for defiling his sister Tamar. Absalom than avenged his sister by killing his half-brother Amnon (v21-29). Thereafter Jonadab reported to David their father that *'only Amnon has died'*. The same friend who was meant to stay with Amnon and grieve with him was the first one to run and report the news to David without any trace of sorrow or remorse for his actions.

May our children never have fake friends like Jonadab.

Rehoboam ignored wise council from the elders, and instead chose to follow his friends' advice. As a result, Rehoboam's kingdom fell as revealed in 1 Kings 12:13.

Rejecting the advice given by elders can lead to costly outcomes and a negative turn in our lives. Proverbs 5:1, 2 and 7 admonishes us:

> *My son, pay attention to my wisdom; lend your ear to my understanding, that you may preserve discretion, and your lips may keep knowledge. Therefore hear me now, my children, and do not depart from the words of my mouth.*

Following our loving Heavenly Father's instruction grants us security through the wisdom and understanding we receive from those who walk closely with God and heed His Voice. Proverbs 4:1-9 reveals:

> *Hear, my children, the instruction of a father, and give attention to know understanding; for I give you good doctrine: Do not forsake my law. When I was my father's son, tender and the only one in the sight of my mother, He also taught me, and said to me:* "**Let your heart retain my words; keep my commands, and live. Get wisdom! Get understanding! Do not forget, nor turn away from the words of my mouth. Do not forsake her, and she will preserve you; love her, and she will keep you. Wisdom is the principal thing; therefore get wisdom. And in all your getting, get understanding.** *Exalt her, and she will promote you; she will bring you honor, when you embrace her. She will place on your head an ornament of grace; a crown of glory she will deliver to you.*"

We also receive the promise of enjoying long life when we obey godly instruction (v10-13, 22-23).

> *Hear, my son, and receive my sayings, and the years of your life will be many. I have taught you in the way of wisdom; I have led you in right paths. When you walk, your steps will not be hindered, and when you run, you will not stumble. Take firm hold of instruction, do not let go; keep her, for she is your life. ...* **For they are life to those who find them, and health to all their flesh**. *Keep your heart with all diligence,*

for out of it spring the issues of life.
(Emphasis mine)

The benefits of following the path of wisdom far outweigh the alternative. Long life, health, success and protection are all benefits of following a godly lifestyle.

You can decree the above verses to yourself as a daily reminder of the promise that will follow you when you obey these words. Let us make them personal:

I enjoy a long life.

I walk in righteous paths and learn the way of wisdom.

When I walk, my steps will not be hindered, and when I run, I will not stumble.

The same sentiment is echoed in Isaiah 40:31.

> *But those who wait on the Lord shall renew their strength; they shall mount up with wings like eagles, they shall run and not be weary, they shall walk and not faint.*

This is your legacy, my friend, as a faithful child of God.

Time to Reflect:

How do your friends add value to your life?

Name 5 ways you add value to your friends' lives.

**Do not be deceived:
"Evil company corrupts good habits."**

(1 Corinthians 15:33)

Chapter Twelve:
Restoring our Focus on Christ

We need to return to the point where we met with Christ Jesus and received our salvation. Altar calls must replace money calls. It is essential for all pastors and ministry leaders to stop gimmicks. For example: selling and buying at the pulpit is not based on the Word of God. Such actions are not pleasing to God.

Once we repent and turn from our wicked ways, we are washed clean by the Blood of Jesus Christ. Walking in the newness of God's love requires daily spiritual and mental cleansing so that we robe ourselves with God's Divine character. Only then will we showcase His nature to others through our lifestyle.

There is a lively Sunday School chorus that talks about the great change since the writer got born again. 1 John 3:1 declares,

> *Behold what manner of love the Father has bestowed on us, that we should be called children of God! Therefore the world does not know us, because it did not know Him.*

As God's beloved children we are the walking mirrors those around us will see and be inspired to know this Christ who lives in us. Let us therefore walk in holiness.

Hold on to the Living Word of God and apply its blueprint as we grow in and display the love of Jesus Christ.

John 13:1-17 relates how Jesus washed His disciples' feet. This act signified spiritual cleansing. Jesus set us the perfect example of loving service that yields fruit for the Kingdom. He further admonished His disciples to do likewise (v12-17).

> *So when He had washed their feet, taken His garments, and sat down again, He said to them, "Do you know what I have done to you?* **You call Me Teacher and Lord, and you say well, for so I am. If I then, your Lord and Teacher, have washed your feet, you also ought to wash one another's feet. For I have given you an example, that you should do as I have done to you.** *Most assuredly, I say to you, a servant is not greater than his master; nor is he who is sent greater than he who sent him. If you know these things, blessed are you if you do them.* (Emphasis mine)

Let every believer tap into God's heartbeat by following the Great Commission Jesus instructed His disciples in Matthew 28:16-20.

> *Then the eleven disciples went away into Galilee, to the mountain which Jesus had appointed for them. When they saw Him, they worshiped Him; but some doubted. And Jesus came and spoke to them, saying, "All authority*

has been given to Me in heaven and on earth. **Go therefore and make disciples of all the nations, baptizing them in the name of the Father and of the Son and of the Holy Spirit, teaching them to observe all things that I have commanded you; and lo, I am with you always, even to the end of the age."** Amen. (Emphasis mine)

Let us set the right foundation so we will be able to stand in the face of challenges in these last days, as Psalm 11:3 declares: *If the foundations are destroyed, what can the righteous do?*

Ephesians 6:10-18 gives us the blueprint to cover ourselves so that we will not falter in our Christian walk. It is essential to remain standing after we have done what is required of us, by equipping ourselves with the whole armor of God.

> *Finally, my brethren, be strong in the Lord and in the power of His might. Put on the whole armor of God, that you may be able to stand against the wiles of the devil. For we do not wrestle against flesh and blood, but against principalities, against powers, against the rulers of the darkness of this age, against spiritual hosts of wickedness in the heavenly places. Therefore take up the whole armor of God, that you may be able to withstand in the evil day, and having done all, to stand.*

Stand therefore, having girded your waist with truth, having put on the breastplate of righteousness, and having shod your feet with the preparation of the gospel of peace; above all, taking the shield of faith with which you will be able to quench all the fiery darts of the wicked one. And take the helmet of salvation, and the sword of the Spirit, which is the word of God; praying always with all prayer and supplication in the Spirit, being watchful to this end with all perseverance and supplication for all the saints.

Let us consider Jonah the servant of God who learned this principle, as recorded in the Old Testament. Jonah repented and was restored to his purpose. God then gave him a second chance and called him to preach deliverance to the inhabitants of Nineveh. We read the account recorded in Jonah 3:1-10:

Now the word of the Lord came to Jonah the second time, saying, "Arise, go to Nineveh, that great city, and preach to it the message that I tell you." **So Jonah arose and went to Nineveh, according to the word of the Lord.** *...Then he cried out and said, "Yet forty days, and Nineveh shall be overthrown!" So the people of Nineveh believed God, proclaimed a fast, and put on sackcloth, from the greatest to the least of them.* **Then word came to the king of Nineveh; and he arose from his throne and laid aside his robe, covered himself with sackcloth and sat**

> *in ashes. And he caused it to be proclaimed and published throughout Nineveh by the decree of the king and his nobles, saying, Let neither man nor beast, herd nor flock, taste anything; do not let them eat, or drink water. But let man and beast be covered with sackcloth, and cry mightily to God; yes, let everyone turn from his evil way and from the violence that is in his hands. Who can tell if God will turn and relent, and turn away from His fierce anger, so that we may not perish?* ***Then God saw their works, that they turned from their evil way; and God relented from the disaster that He had said He would bring upon them, and He did not do it***. (Emphasis mine)

Dressing in sackcloth signified the king's humility before the Lord. Our obedience touches the heart of God and creates breakthroughs for the people the Holy Spirit sends us to guide and deliver by faith.

When the church is in tune with God's heartbeat, nothing the enemy tries will succeed as Isaiah 59:19 declares:

> *So shall they fear the name of the Lord from the west, and His glory from the rising of the sun;* ***when the enemy comes in like a flood, the Spirit of the Lord will lift up a standard against him***. (Emphasis mine)

Possessing our Inheritance in God

It is time for every believer to claim back what belongs to us. Obadiah 1:17 reveals, *"But on Mount Zion there shall be deliverance, and there shall be holiness; the house of Jacob shall possess their possessions."*

I decree and declare that the body of Christ will be holy. We will possess our possessions. This means that we will have voices in the government where leaders will listen to us. God's purpose will be fulfilled in our lives, in our communities, in our workplaces, in our countries and in our continents as we proclaim the Word of God wherever He has called us to stand in the gap. We will live to declare and possess our inheritance in Christ Jesus.

Therefore, my dear brother and sister in the Lord, do not fear or be intimidated when the enemy tries to scare you. He has no power over you because God has raised a higher standard against the enemy. God will deliver you and uplift you as you remain firmly rooted in the Word of God.

Proclaim the Word over every situation and stand strong in your faith. Resist the enemy and he will flee from you, in the mighty Name of Jesus.

Time to Reflect:

In what areas has God called you to serve?

Name one area you want God to uplift you and showcase His glory in your life.

Pray. Ask for God's Divine guidance and the opportunity to be effective in your calling.

Search me, O God, and know my heart; try me, and know my anxieties; and see if there is any wicked way in me, and lead me in the way everlasting.

(Psalm 139:23-24)

Chapter Thirteen:
Prodigal Believers Link to the Parables

In the three parables we discussed earlier, have you considered what each percentage of what was lost represents?

The parable of *The Lost Sheep* represents *one percent* of the one hundred sheep the farmer had. Since only one was lost, ninety-nine sheep were safe. Jesus said the farmer rejoiced over the one sheep who was once lost and restored to the fold. This means every single life is significant in God's eyes. His loving heart yearns for every lost soul to be restored to the Father.

Next, *The Lost Coin* represents *ten percent*. The woman initially had ten coins. After she lost one coin, she lit a lamp, swept the floor and tirelessly searched the room until she found her lost coin. She then called her friends to rejoice with her over her restored coin. Finding the ten percent was a big deal for the woman. Likewise, we should also value and give thanks for the many blessings God has placed into our hands.

Finally, *The Lost Son* represents a massive *fifty percent* of the total. The father had two sons and one asked for his inheritance. When the prodigal son went off and squandered what he had not worked for, he failed to realise that he was mindlessly diminishing his inheritance.

The father's decision to give his son the inheritance in the first place demonstrates God's love and desire to give us free will. Sometimes we act foolishly like the young man, by not honouring what God has blessed us with. Yet our loving Father still chooses to forgive us and restore us into right relationship with Himself when we return to Him in repentance and humility.

From the parable of *The Prodigal Son*, we learned that the Prodigal believer gets to mingle with the pigs. This is compared with being yoked with unbelievers who do not feel bad when they sin.

The heart that fears God is still intact, so the prodigal believer reasoned saying: *In my father's house I have anything I want. Yet here I am eating the same food as the pigs.*

Pigs are unclean and love indulging in dirty activities. That is their happiest place. Likewise, the prodigal believer indulges in things that are contrary to what God has designed for him. Deep down the prodigal is torn between walking in the ways of the world and following God's precepts, yet there is truth in his heart.

Proverbs 22:6 admonishes us, *Train up a child in the way he should go, and when he is old he will not depart from it.* While living the dirty lifestyle, the prodigal son must have reflected on his previous lifestyle before and the present state in which he found himself. He may then have concluded that returning to his family home had better benefits than the reckless choice he had made.

The prodigal youngster may have recalled his parents' advice on the importance of living a godly or honorable life. His reasoning and reflecting on his current situation demonstrate that the fear of God was still in him, hence his return to his father's house with humility.

What activities do unbelievers indulge in?

Many unbelievers engage in drugs, drinking, promiscuity, worldly music, wrong company, clubbing, and more. Friday night is typically named 'club night'. Meanwhile, for believers, Friday night is the time for 'night vigil', a special time when believers set aside to seek the Lord's face and connect with His heart and desire for their spiritual growth.

The devil loves to do things that are contrary to the Lord's standards with the sole intention of confusing and derailing the Lord's children. The devil's aim is to divert the prodigal son's destiny, calling, and purpose.

For example, a young female worshipper can easily be swayed and derailed by a prodigal son. He may convince her to meet with him at the time she should be attending worship rehearsals, church services and other spiritually enhancing activities.

The prodigal son felt unworthy to receive his previous place of honour as a natural son and was happy to be welcomed back and even treated as one of the servants.,

The father however demonstrated God's love by honouring and restoring his son to his rightful position before his entire household.

We can draw strength from knowing that we have the freedom to reconnect to God for *the joy of the Lord is our strength.* (Nehemiah 8:10)

Have you wondered what might have contributed to the prodigal son's wandering away from following the Lord? Although he did what he was not supposed to be doing by prematurely asking for his inheritance, thankfully the son realized the folly of his unwise choices and decided to return home.

When the sleeping church disrobes themselves, they become an easy target to be attacked by the enemy. Let us be grateful for the mercy of God which restores sinners.

Whatever the prodigal's unclean state, God is ready to cleanse every spot of dirt and filth, waiting patiently to restore the believer to his former glory. Psalm 139:23-24 encourages us to ask God to search our hearts and cleanse us of all unrighteousness.

> *Search me, O God, and know my heart; try me, and know my anxieties; and see if there is any wicked way in me, and lead me in the way everlasting.*

Take a moment and pray the above verse by faith.

Love Them Back to the Fold

Jesus taught His disciples the importance of faithfully evangelizing and acknowledging the joy of a lost sinner who repents and turns away from wickedness. There is much rejoicing in heaven over one soul who repents and turns from their wicked ways than from a hundred who have on need of repentance, according to Luke 15:10.

What can you do to help bring those who have lost their way back into the fold? They may think their options are all exhausted. However, we should remember that God always has a soft spot for every person who is ready to return to Him. He will exchange every unclean life for a life of integrity and honour. Above all, God's *love covers a multitude of sins* (1 Peter 4:8).

The prodigal son's father waited anxiously by the window, peering in the distance every day. He hoped to see his beloved son walk up the path as he returned home from his freedom stint after getting his inheritance.

When a sinner is swayed by the world's agenda, they do not realise the folly of stepping out of the grace of God. Asking for God's mercy is the first step to the prodigal returning home.

Jesus came to bind up the brokenhearted and restore us to Himself, as Isaiah 61:1-3 records:

> *"The Spirit of the Lord God is upon Me, because the Lord has anointed Me to preach good tidings to the poor; He has sent Me to heal (bind up) the*

brokenhearted, to proclaim liberty to the captives, and the opening of the prison to those who are bound; to proclaim the acceptable year of the Lord, and the day of vengeance of our God; to comfort all who mourn, to console those who mourn in Zion, to give them beauty for ashes, the oil of joy for mourning, the garment of praise for the spirit of heaviness; that they may be called trees of righteousness, the planting of the Lord, that He may be glorified."

Every prodigal believer needs to come to our senses and accept the gift of building a lasting relationship with our Redeemer and Lord. Where did we go wrong? We need to do some soul-searching and reflecting, to get back on track with God's direction and purpose.

Time to Reflect:

Pause for a moment and consider:

1. Are you where God wants you to be in the ministry?

2. Are you serving your gifts fully?

If you are not fully aligned with God's will you need to reflect on what He has impressed on your heart about your calling and purpose.

3. Are you struggling with past hurts from being let down or disappointed by others? Do you have any regrets? Release the hurt and regrets and ask God to heal you as you forgive yourself.

4. Choose to return to your Creator and ask Him to direct your path so that you will be fruitful where He has planted you.

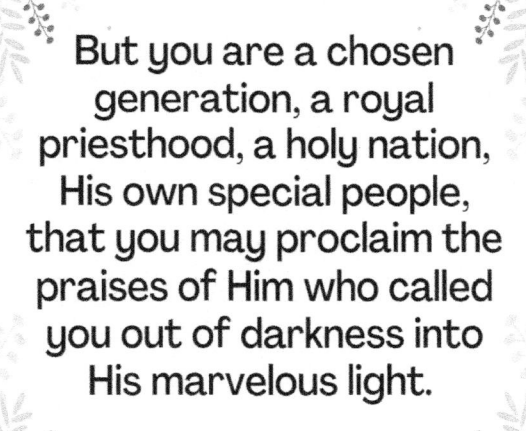

> But you are a chosen generation, a royal priesthood, a holy nation, His own special people, that you may proclaim the praises of Him who called you out of darkness into His marvelous light.
>
> (1 Peter 2:9)

Chapter Fourteen:
The Glorious Church

Irrespective of our weakness, God's agenda will be made known. Let us compare the lives of Samson and Samuel.

Scholars made it known that Samson was a legendary Israelite warrior and judge. He was also an ordained leader. An angel appeared to Samson's parents to foretell what he could and could not do. When he was of age, they disclosed these instructions to him, along with what he was allowed to eat and what was forbidden. His parents also instructed Samson on who to marry. From this we can conclude, even without reading the Book of Proverbs, that there is a specific meal provided for the children of God to eat.

Proverbs 21:17b states, *He that loveth wine and oil shall not be rich.* Proverbs 31:4-5 (KJV) also warns us, *It is not for kings… to drink wine; nor for princes strong drink: lest they drink, and forget the law, and pervert the judgment of any of the afflicted.*

Look at that. Don't just read the Scriptures. You will do well to also focus on the instructions. It is not wise for kings to partake of strong drink. *Who are the present-day kings?* The believers in Christ! This confirmation is found in Revelation 1:5-6:

and from Jesus Christ, the faithful witness, the firstborn from the dead, and the ruler over the kings of the earth. To Him who loved us and washed us from our sins in His own blood, and has made us kings and priests to His God and Father, to Him be glory and dominion forever and ever. Amen.

The believers are the **kings** and **priests** whose manual is The Holy Bible. They obey the precepts their Creator has laid out for godly living and spiritual growth.

When you follow Samson's life closely, you will discover how he worked against the template he was given to rule as a judge over the house of Israel. Samson allowed himself to be deceived because he was not conscious of his sacred being. You may know the story. Many people might be thinking Samson is in hell fire. However, I do not believe this is true because his name was recorded in the Book of Hebrews Chapter 11 as among those who won.

Consider this: Are we not causing more atrocities beyond what Samson did? I believe that "*The Best of Man is Still a Man.*" That you did not fulfil God's agenda over your life never made God's words return to Him in vain. Remember, you have a replacement.

Samuel's birth was miraculous. His mother made a vow to God who then blessed her with baby Samuel, after which she offered him back to the Lord.

Samuel's ways were right before the Lord; he took the position of Hophni and Phinehas, the two sons of Eli who did wrong in the sight of the Lord. We read in 1 Samuel 3:19: *"So Samuel grew, and the Lord was with him and let none of his words fall to the ground."* Samuel followed God's direction. When we follow Divine direction, we structure our ways to the path God wants us to follow.

Another example is Absalom, King David's son, who killed his brother then ran away into exile. When David sent for him, Absalom returned home but his behavior did not match his father's. He might have learnt the negative traits from Geshur, the land he ran to after killing his brother Amnon (2 Samuel 13:38).

Consider the instruction God has laid on your heart to fulfil. How are you following it through?

Do not allow the enemy to derail your life's purpose by making you too busy to deliver what God has assigned for you to do in building the Kingdom. Do not allow yourself to be replaced because of disobedience, as Eli's sons Hophni and Phinehas were.

May the Lord grant you strength, confidence, patience and perseverance to see His Word in your life come to pass, in the Matchless Name of Jesus Christ.

Ponder this.

Samson destroyed the Philistines without taking anything from them to use as treasure. He was indeed a *king* and *priest*!

The Bible **also** records that David was a man after God's heart.

Remember, none of God's Word will go unfulfilled.

Beyond being a man after God's heart, God made you His own.

Claim what 1 Peter 2:9 declares about who you are in Christ Jesus: *a **chosen generation**, a **royal priesthood**, a **holy nation**, His own **special people**.* Moreover, God has chosen you to *proclaim the praises of Him who called you out of darkness into His marvellous light*.

As you have received the Light of God through His saving grace, share it abroad and do your part to restore lost souls to their loving Creator.

Christians, Wake up!

The hour of our revival is around the corner. What are you doing that is not of God? Do away with it before the day catches you unaware.

Time to Reflect:

Are you worthy of the accolades you have received?

What clear instructions has God laid on your heart to fulfil?

How are you following it through?

Commit to praying for Divine guidance and strength to fulfil your Divine purpose. The Holy Spirit will back you up as you ask Him by faith.

> Trust in the Lord with all your heart, and lean not on your own understanding; in all your ways acknowledge Him, and He shall direct your paths.
>
> (Proverbs 3:5-6)

Chapter Fifteen:
Return to Your First Love

The final Book of the New Testament outlines the importance of returning to our First Love as believers who want to walk in and display the Light of God.

Revelation 2:2-7 describes The Loveless Church.

> "To the angel of the church of Ephesus write, 'These things says He who holds the seven stars in His right hand, who walks in the midst of the seven golden lampstands: "I know your works, your labor, your patience, and that you cannot bear those who are evil. And you have tested those who say they are apostles and are not, and have found them liars; and you have persevered and have patience, and have labored for My name's sake and have not become weary. **Nevertheless I have this against you, that you have left your first love. Remember therefore from where you have fallen; repent and do the first works, or else I will come to you quickly and remove your lampstand from its place—unless you repent.** But this you have, that you hate the deeds of the Nicolaitans, which I also hate. "He who has an ear, let him hear what the Spirit says to the churches. To him who

overcomes I will give to eat from the tree of life, which is in the midst of the Paradise of God." '
(Emphasis mine)

Let us begin by answering these crucial questions:

What has changed?

What has stopped the Glory of God from manifesting?

What should we do to bring back the Glory of God?

The first thing is to repent. Let us acknowledge that we have sinned and fallen short of the Glory of God (Romans 3:23). The Bible states in Isaiah 59:1-2 that sin has separated us from the Glory of God. God cannot perform His acts among us or through us when we continue in sin.

What sins have we as the Church committed that we need to repent of? (Revelation 2:4-5)

What things we are doing or failing to do that are preventing revival?

In the days of Smith Wigglesworth, Kathryn Kuhlman and Billy Graham the early church gave themselves fully to God. They served God with all their heart and the church multiplied numerically and spiritually. Many came to the Lord through the disciples.

The Gospel was all about Jesus and the Good News of salvation. However, in today's church many people are preaching different things apart from the Gospel message of the Kingdom of God. Many are making altar calls for other things besides calling for people to be saved.

Are we nurturing the new believer?

I believe we also need to have a new believer's class; this is very important. After a person has received the Lord as their personal Saviour, they need proper follow up.

When we were born again in the late eighties, our Pastors, sisters and brothers followed up with us by teaching us the importance of our decision. They guided us in the steps to take to help us grow as believers in God. These steps helped our new journey greatly; as a result, many of the saints who were born again in the eighties and nineties had a strong solid foundation.

How can we nurture spiritual growth for longevity in the Christian walk?

I think that money issues and messages focused on building altars should not be introduced to new believers before they understand the importance of salvation. I know of many who fell back into worldly ways and are no longer in church because they did not understand the issue of 'seed time'. I believe when the seed giving message comes at the right time, the Holy Spirit will have His way of teaching new believers how to grow in the Lord.

In Acts 6, the apostles had to choose some of the mature brothers to serve at the tables as they spread the Good News to the world. For example, Stephen was stoned for his faith. He served steadfastly as a mature follower of the Word of God. If new believers are not taught the Word of God, we might end up with a lot of prodigal sons and daughters who go away and never reason to themselves, because they lack the right foundation.

What stopped the Glory of God?

What happened to the move of God, signs and wonders and the revival?

One of the main obstacles is **pride**. Pride took the place of humility. Many started out very humble, yet when they saw the Glory of God manifest in their lives, their egos puffed up and they started exalting themselves with big titles and great names. As they massaged their big egos, they forgot their humble beginnings. They forgot the *Blesser* and started focusing on the *blessing*.

Psalm 147:6 declares: *The Lord lifts up the humble; He casts the wicked down to the ground.* When God has lifted you up do not forget your humble beginning. Let me share a personal testimony to illustrate this.

Shortly after we started our ministry, a woman of God came from America and ministered to our congregation for two days. On the third day she received a phone call from another minister. Shortly after, she left and told us she was a great servant of God. She also stated that she would not continue ministering to a small congregation as she had a large membership at her local church. This really disturbed me because the people we invited to our event would think that we used the preacher's image or name to invite them.

It is not good to have class divisions and levels within the Christian family, for example grouping ourselves in terms of church membership or how many people attend our services. Often when you are inviting someone, they will want to know the number of people you have invited and roughly how many people you are expecting to attend. Many church leaders will also want to know beforehand if you will be preaching, will you be asking for a special offering? The preacher will also want to know how much you would want him to raise and how much he would be getting.

All this is missing the whole point of witnessing to unbelievers. The purpose should be to win souls for Christ, not to enrich the preacher's pockets, as has become the norm in many modern-day churches and crusades.

We have stopped hearing from God. We are holding meetings that God did not ordain or ask for. Because of this we end up having to ask the congregation to give great seed offerings so that God would bless them in double or triple portion. We invite men and women to minister in meetings which we planned by ourselves, without first consulting God through prayer, to know His mind on the matter.

If God asks you to go on a mission, He will give the provision. You will relax and see the goodness of the Lord in the land of the living. When God speaks, you do not struggle or worry, because He takes full control.

The pressure on some churches have made some men and women of God to get into debt by hiring big conference halls, paying for expensive flight tickets, and accommodating preachers in big hotels. All this just to fit in with other churches which are holding conferences and inviting great men of God. Smaller churches feel the need to emulate more established congregations which have the resources to foot these large conferences at great expense.

Incurring huge bills just to fit in with the 'Joneses' was never in God's plan for His Church to grow. Such ill thought-out practices make church members pledge a lot of money that they cannot afford. As a result, many worshippers end up running away from church due to embarrassment. The church leaders then turn to preaching about building altars as their way to offset bills. They focus on *"giving God your Isaac, for God loves a cheerful giver";* very biblical, but "what is the catch" to offset the bill?

A preacher once asked me when I was going to have a women's conference. She was surprised when I told her we were not planning to. Our last women's conference had been two years prior, and we had no immediate plans to hold another. I also told her that nowhere did the Bible indicate that we needed to have a yearly meeting. I explained to the minister that we preferred to walk the streets doing evangelism rather than inviting born-again believers every year to come and hear new preachers.

Most of the meetings many churches hold yearly do not target the non-believers. Moreover, whenever non-believers attend, no altar call is made. May God help the body of Christ. If we want to see God in our midst we need to turn back to God in humility.

Let us return to our 'First Love' and let Proverbs 3:5-6 be our anchor Scripture. *"Trust in the Lord with all your heart, and lean not on your own understanding; in all your ways acknowledge Him, and He shall direct your paths."*

What should we do to bring back the Glory of God?

First, we need to humble ourselves and ask God for a Spirit of discernment. Jesus instructed the believers to wait until they were filled with the power of the Holy Spirit (Acts 1:4). Jesus called the Holy Spirit a "Gift". The Church now needs to be re-filled by the Power of the Holy Spirit beyond just Speaking in Tongues.

The next thing we need is Divine Direction. When we have a clear spiritual connection, our spiritual eyes will see, and our spiritual ears will hear what the Lord is speaking to us.

Gaining spiritual discernment will guide the Church to know and distinguish the wolves from the true sheep. In today's church there are many wolves pretending to be sheep. We have good actors who can act like true believers; they talk and try to walk like true believers and yet they are Satan's cousins or agents.

Church members should not be transferring or moving from one church to another unless they are relocating to a considerable distance. This is what has been happening with members moving from place to place, from one church congregation to another. For example, a new pastor or church in a certain area may invite local people to help with ushering, which then turns into a transfer. Some even offer to pay the instrumentalist so that they continue to attend the service where they play and get paid; if they are not paid the musician moves to another church.

The way the church is moving today is not how the early church operated. The modern-day church has lost its true calling and purpose as God intended for it. Now is the time for each of us to do our part to restore God's order and plan for His Church. Let us uncover how to take our rightful positions by the grace of God.

How to Restore the Church's True Calling and Purpose

#1. When you notice a member from another church move to your local church's leadership or congregation and you are aware that they are from another pastor's parish, ask questions to learn what their intention is. Carefully and wisely handle the matter by talking to your trusted pastor friend about the issue. Always focus on the person's soul as you consider how to handle the concern with deep care.

#2. Be mindful of the individual's level of maturity. Let us also ensure that we teach about the importance of building a strong foundation. When the foundation is secure, we will not hear of untimely church transfers because the foundation and structure will be solid.

#3. We should also encourage home cell groups and Bible study attendance; these small groups are what build the church. When the church is grounded, we will have believers who can pray and attend weekday services. This is how church members will grow into committed and mature believers.

#4. Do some research on what church growth strategies to employ from men and women of God who are making it. Are they following godly principle in their church growth?

#5. Let us also stop criticizing pastors based on what they are wearing, what they are driving or the houses they are living in. Instead, we should judge them by their fruit; this is scriptural.

#6. Uplift pastors by sharing the spiritual gifts God has bestowed upon your life. Remember the Church is a body of believers who are designed to work in one accord.

Time for Action.

Do you know your calling within the Body of Christ?

How are you applying your spiritual gifts to empower growth in other believers within your church, home, workplace and community?

In what other ways can you serve out your physical and spiritual gifts?

Conclusion

All three parables illustrate firstly, the infinite love and mercy of God. The Lost Sheep, The Lost Coin, and The Prodigal Son teach of the Lord's love and care for us all. We learn that no human being ever goes beyond the Saviour's care. The Lord came to *"seek and to save the lost"* (Luke 19:10). His command to us is also *"seek and you shall find"* (Matthew 7:7).

In the parable of The Lost Coin, we have the picture of a woman seeking for a treasure which she once had but lost. She knows that it is in the house somewhere, and she also believes that if she searches diligently, she will find it. Our human nature causes us to dislike losing something we once had. Even though it may be a very small loss, the loss still disturbs us. If we had given it away, we should probably have scarcely missed it. We might even feel better in the knowledge that someone else is enjoying it. However, when we lose it without knowing how, the loss irks us, then we make every effort to recover the lost treasure.

The same can be seen in the way the prodigal son's father believed he was alive and had high expectations of seeing him again. This is unlike Israel upon being told that Joseph was dead, his spirit was crushed, and no further expectation was given.

Based on these parables, every believer should ask:

Have I lost anything of value that I once possessed?

Have I lost that condition of implicit faith and trusting confidence in my Heavenly Father which I once had?

Am I submerged in the things of the world, buried beneath the dust of worldliness, folly, and pride?

Whatever we have lost, the Lord's wish is for us to find it again. We only lose truth when we do not practice it. If we do not practice the Truth and heavenly principles in our minds and daily lives, that becomes the beginning of the believer's downfall.

The Lost Coin is still in the house and our parable tells us exactly what to do to find it. First light a candle and sweep the house. The **house** is our mind or soul within which all our treasures reside. Our mind is a dwelling place where we store many things. Consider how many things are also lost within the confines of the mind.

The **candle** that lights our search is Truth from the Lord.

Your word is a lamp to my feet and a light to my path (Psalm 119:105). From Him proceeds all Truth. God's Word is the Light of the world.

Regardless of one's age, whether as a child, adult, scholar, or minister of the Gospel of Jesus, everyone who receives and understands the Word of Truth is lighting a candle. By this light each one can then navigate life's challenges guided by the Light of God.

The deeper question we need to ask is:

For what purpose are we lighting the candle?

Is it to sweep the house and find what we have lost, or merely to show others how clever and superior we are? Are we learning the Truth as we should, in order that by its Light we may purify our own souls and be better instruments of the Lord in helping others?

No lesson is really of use to us if it does not help us to advance further in finding and building others in Truth.

I pray that the lessons you have learned in this book will help you discover how to return to Christ as you seek His Divine plan for your life.

Are you a church leader seeking resources to nurture growth in your flock? You can use this instructional book in your cell groups, Bible Study sessions, home study or as part of a discipleship training whether online or offline.

May God continually bless your ministry, walk and service in His Vineyard.

Joyfully in Christ's service,

Pastor Lillian Orinda

Connect with the author at: **https://newlifedbc.org/**

> Likewise, I say to you, there is joy in the presence of the angels of God over one sinner who repents.
>
> (Luke 15:10)

About the Author

Pastor Lillian A Orinda is the co-founder and associate pastor of New Life Destiny Baptist Church, based in London UK. She passionately shares her faith and skills within the community focusing on evangelism, Unique Ladies Ministry, youth and church growth.

Pastor Lillian won an Unsung Hero Award from the Kenya Community Rebuild (KCR) network for her service in the community. She holds a Bachelor of Arts degree in Ministerial Theology.

The author ministers with her husband Reverend Walter Orinda and they are blessed with many children who are their joy and delight.

Connect with the author at: **https://newlifedbc.org/**

God bless you.

Pastor Lillian Orinda

You can help spread the word by sharing this manual's ISBN: **9798387509797** with your connections who are seeking a spiritual transformation.

Printed in Great Britain
by Amazon